Roy Moffat

Anna Minette Darling

~ Margaret Moffat?

Dibbie Appleton — who once comforted me
when I complained of "my book" going
to committee. Thank goodness it did — it
is so much the richer for so many minds &
memories & talents! Enjoy Dib

For Sandy —

Joan Niles

Dorothy J. Eastmure

# PENLAKE

## REFLECTIONS ON PENINSULA LAKE

*Children rafting at Penlake.*
– Courtesy Nancy Moffat Scarth

*This book is dedicated to our friends and ancestors who introduced us to Penlake, shared their memories, and helped us to value ours; and to our children that they may cherish these memories and create their own in the future.*

*Once upon a time...*
*Dibbie Spurr in front of her grandmother Brown's cottage in 1940.*
– Courtesy I.S. Appleton

# PENLAKE

## REFLECTIONS ON PENINSULA LAKE

A BOSTON MILLS PRESS BOOK

Stoddart

*The* Algonquin *in the canal between Fairy and Peninsula lakes.*
– Courtesy Irwin Schultz
*Preceding page: The annual "Greasy or Slippery Pole" event at the Springsyde regatta*
*prior to the dock reconstruction of 1916.*
– Courtesy T.L. Moffat IV

Canadian Cataloguing in Publication Data

Main entry under title:
Penlake
ISBN 1–55046–096–X

1. Peninsula Lake (Muskoka, Ont.) – History.
2. Peninsula Lake (Muskoka, Ont.) – Social
Life and customs.
I. Peninsula Lake Association. Historical
Committee.

FC3095.P45P45 1993    971.3'6
C94-930263-5
F1059.5.P45P45 1993

© Peninsula Lake Association.
Design and Typography by Daniel Crack,
Kinetics Design & Illustration
Printed in Canada

First published in 1994 by
Stoddart Publishing Co. Limited
34 Lesmill Road
Toronto, Canada
M3B 2T6

A BOSTON MILLS PRESS BOOK
The Boston Mills Press
132 Main Street
Erin, Ontario
N0B 1T0

The publisher gratefully acknowledges the
support of the Canada Council, Ontario
Ministry of Culture and Communications,
Ontario Arts Council and Ontario Publishing
Centre in the development of writing and
publishing in Canada.

# CONTENTS

# PREFACE

The original mandate of the Peninsula Lake Association's Historical Committee was to research the history of Peninsula Lake and to identify the donors of the many regatta trophies. In so doing, the committee has gathered extensive information about the lake, and the lives and achievements of its pioneers and cottagers. Indeed, so much material has been accumulated that it is too voluminous for one book!

The committee decided to publish this book describing the history of the lake, area landmarks, and the spirit of community. In highlighting the memories of yesteryear, we hope to give readers a taste of life here in the late 1800s and early 1900s.

We want to thank the Peninsula Lake Association for its confidence in our venture and for providing seed money. We are indebted to all those who responded to the 1988 questionnaire, willingly agreed to be interviewed, and contributed valuable information, photographs, and articles.

Our dedicated committee consists of Isabelle "Dibbie" Spurr Appleton (*ISA*), Dorothy Mansell Eastmure (*DME*), Brenda Darling Gilmour (*BDG*), Margaret (Mrs. Norman) Moffat (*MEM*), Robert Moffat (*RDM*), and Jessie Macpherson Stuart (*JMS*). Much-needed assistance came from William Charlton, Russell Eastmure, Margaret (Mrs. Robert) Moffat, T. Lang Moffat IV, and Joan VanDuzer.

The committee extends a special thank-you to our hardworking committee editor, Joan Miles; our helpful facilitator and consulting editor, Ian Gilmour; typists Alexa and Ramona Gilmour; and our publisher, John Denison, for his advice and encouragement.

Sincere gratitude to all,

Anna Mirrette Campbell Darling (*AMD*)
Chairperson, Historical Committee
Peninsula Lake Association

# ACKNOWLEDGMENTS

We are also indebted to the following individuals for their help: Les Ackerman, Robert Brenciaglia, Sylvia Hurst-Brown, Jeanette Shaw Demydas, Maureen Shaw Hammond, Gladys Barnes Lazarus, William C. Mansell, Niall MacKay, and Mr. and Mrs. James Walker of Walker's Lake. We greatly appreciate the contribution of the late Rev. J.K. Moffat for sharing his detailed knowledge of boats. Finally we gratefully acknowledge the following organizations:

Aben Graphics
The Boston Mills Press
Canada Post: Catherine Taylor, Media Relations; Lorraine Belanger; Ida Sequeira
Canada Post Museum: Diane Martineau, Reference and Research Officer,
    Documentary Art and Photography Division
Canada Post, Archives Division
National Archives of Canada: Thomas Hillman, Archivist
    Economic Transportation Unit
    State, Military and Transportation Records
    Government Archives Division
    National Archives of Canada
    Historical Resources Branch
Employment and Immigration Canada:
    C.J.S. Projects Unit, Andrew Hudson, Barrie, Ontario
*Huntsville Forester*
Huntsville Public Library
Muskoka Pioneer Village
Ontario Ministry of the Environment
Royal Conservatory of Music, Toronto
Technology Transfer Ltd.
Toronto Mendelssohn Choir

## Evening Rhapsody

*When evening comes and all is still*
*I hear the ripple of the rill*
*The tinkering bells of drowsy sheep*
*And grazing cows in pastures deep*
*The setting sun with paintbrush bold*
*Has brushed the sky with red and gold*
*The hum of motors on the lake*
*As o'er the water skiers skate*
*The rhythmic dip of blade and oar*
*The water lapping on the shore*
*Out on the meadows breezes play*
*And waft the scent of new mown hay*

*Belva Hill*

# THE NAME OF THE LAKE

ALTHOUGH the Grand Trunk Railroad advertised "hay fever free" air in Muskoka and called our lake Peninsular Lake, in 1922 the government set up Penlake Post Office at North Portage. Over the years our lake has been known as Peninsula, Peninsular, Penn Lake, Pen Lake, and Penlake. Most cottagers prefer Penlake.

*DME*

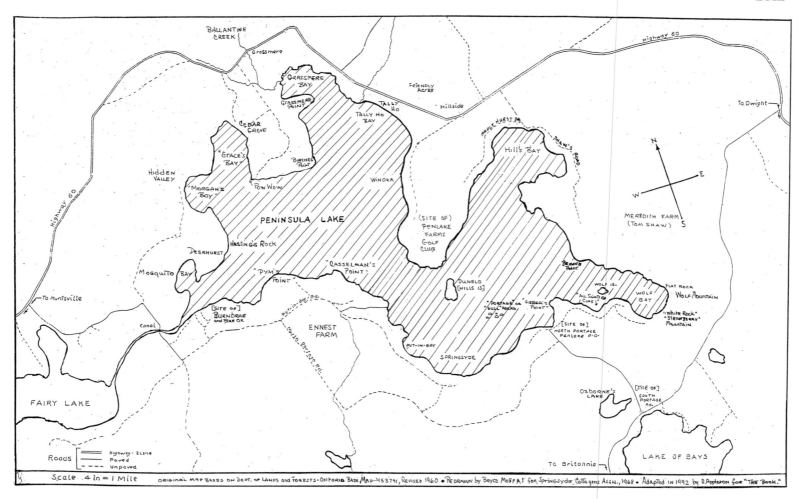

Scale .4 In = 1 Mile — ORIGINAL MAP BASED ON DEPT. OF LANDS AND FORESTS · ONTARIO BASE MAP 453791, REVISED 1960 · REDRAWN by Bryce Moffat for Springsyde Cottagers Assn., 1968 · Adapted in 1992 by D. Appleton for "THE BOOK."

*~ Satellite view of Penlake ~*
– Canadian Department of Energy, Mines and Resources map

*The* Ramona *at the Mary River locks.*
– Courtesy Don Marshall

# EARLY HISTORY

## INTRODUCTION

FROM MARY'S LAKE, the two men paddled down Fairy Lake into a wide creek that flowed almost due east. At times, the creek was so shallow that the canoe's occupants had to pole. When their heavy load made the going too difficult, they got out and pushed. Eventually the stream opened into another crystal-clear body of water, the natural beauty of which astounded the men.

They took two days to paddle around it. The irregular shoreline was divided by a prominent piece of land jutting southward toward a large central island. They named the lake Peninsula and the island Donnel, possibly after one of them. Today the island is known as Isle Dunelg.

The year was 1853. The canoeists were the first surveyors to chart what are now called the Huntsville Lakes: Mary, Fairy, Peninsula, and Vernon.

The passing of the Free Land Grant and Homesteads Act in 1868 opened up the Muskoka wilderness, named after the Rama chief Mesqua Ukee. The act said that any man eighteen or older could lay claim to a hundred acres. If he cleared at least fifteen of them, built a habitable dwelling, and lived in it for six months, he would receive the deed to his claim in five years.

The first white man to venture into the area was a trapper named Cann, who built a crude shanty near the river. More arrivals soon followed, and they established a small village. One of the settlers was George Hunt, who not only saw that a road was completed into the village, but persuaded the government to open a post office. Not surprisingly, the settlement was named Huntsville.

While trapping was an interest, the first settlers came primarily to farm; a few arrived simply for the adventure. They were followed by lumbermen, drawn by the rich timber of the shore. The first sawmill was erected in Huntsville in 1885.

The construction of locks between Mary and Fairy lakes in 1875, coupled with the dredging of the canal between Fairy and Peninsula lakes in 1888, made Penlake accessible to tourists and cottagers. They came in search of peace, tranquillity, and the excitement of roughing it. In 1896 Charles Waterhouse, an Englishman, established a fine fishing lodge on Penlake near the canal. He named it Deerhurst Inn. Several families who stayed at the inn fell in love with the lake and sought out Crown properties of their own. Clusters of cottages appeared at Springbank (now called Springsyde) and Winoka.

*The "Hupmobile" (circa 1925) belonging to James Moffat.*
– Courtesy Nancy Moffat Scarth

*Postcard picturing the canal road bridge near Huntsville, Muskoka.*

With the aid of small government loans, settlers put in colonization roads such as the one built by the Hill family around 1870. It skirted the shores of Fairy and Peninsula lakes as far east as Hillside.

Many early cottagers came by train, for the roads were narrow and rough; passage by horse-drawn coach or automobile was not easy. For those coming great distances, the trip to the cottage was made in stages, often requiring several days to complete.

The people of the First Nations, who'd known our lake long before the white man came, sold their wares to the early cottagers. Beautiful baskets made of sweet grass and decorated with porcupine quills are still found in a good number of the older cottages.

Over the years Peninsula Lake has been completely settled; many would say oversettled. Fifth-generation cottagers continue to flock here each summer. Now that some cottages are winterized and access made possible by snowmobile, or plowed roads, many also come up in winter.

In 1987 the historical committee was formed by the Peninsula Lake Association to record the history of the lake since the 1850s. We have endeavoured to convey the pioneering spirit of the early cottagers and to capture the flavour of those years. We hope that we have succeeded.

*ISA*

## LOGGING

Logging was an important industry on the shores of Peninsula Lake for many years. Timber was collected into large booms and hauled to the mill in Huntsville by the little tug *Phoenix*.

There is evidence of several major log chutes around the lake, and sunken logs still lurk close to the shores. One such site was on the hill where Ralph and Betty Jane Thompson's cottage stands today.

An old logging camp stood on the Springsyde property now owned by Kim Edwards Simpson. The original cabin walls can still be seen on the inside of the present cottage.

The Golden Lumber Company, owned by E.S. Brooks, once operated a sawmill on what is now Doug Woollings' land. The original concrete engine mounts can be seen on the neighbouring property of William Luke.

Brooks also had a sawmill in the bay, on land that Verne Oke's cottage stands on today. Both Grassmere and Hill's Bay were used as collection areas to gather logs for booms.

*AMD*

*Logging on Penlake.*
– Courtesy Irwin Schultz

*The old iron bridge over the canal, before it was replaced in 1990.*
– Courtesy Don Marshall

# THE HILLS OF HILLSIDE

In 1867 the Reverend Robert Norton Hill was serving a Methodist parish in Schomberg, Ontario. In that year the Wesleyans and the Methodists merged, creating a surplus of ministers for the church. Rev. Hill had met a Mr. McMurray, who had settled near Bracebridge at South Falls. Hill came north to visit McMurray and to seek land for his four sons. He also had two daughters.

Although the terrain at South Falls was level, the soil was too sandy. The next day Hill walked to Bracebridge and was disappointed again. Searching for better land farther north, he eventually reached Lake Vernon, where he claimed eight hundred acres. He returned to Bracebridge and dreamed of land "beside a lake with a point jutting out in the water with an island beside it." Inquiring if such a piece of land existed, the minister was taken to Peninsula Lake. There he claimed a large piece of property matching his dream, and he cancelled his earlier claim.

In the spring of 1868 Rev. Hill and his family built a cabin on his land. The first permanent settlers east of Huntsville, they took up residence in the spring of 1869. The trail Hill blazed from Huntsville to his property, once known as Hill's Trace, is now Highway 60.

In 1874 Hill moved a mile east along the shore and constructed a house near

*Rowland Hill family, 1916, in a skiff. Left to right: Rowland Hill, Mrs. Hill, Belva, Annie, Carolyn, Gordon (child), and Leonard Hill.*

– Hill photo, courtesy Jean Dunlop

14

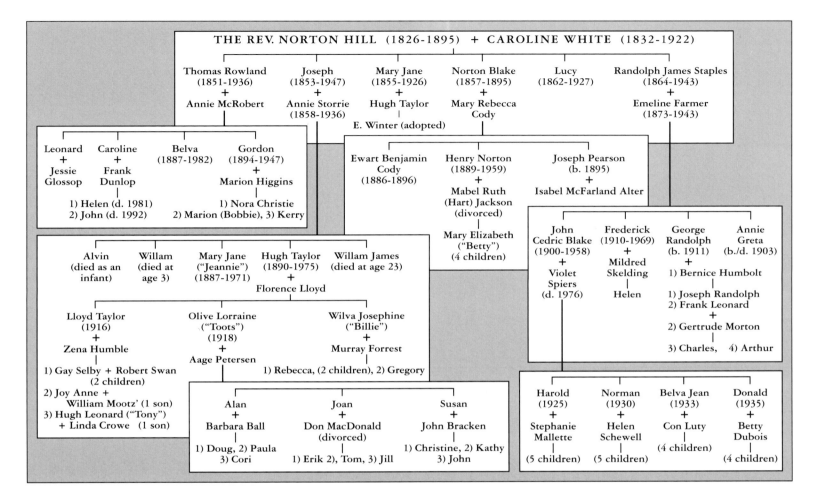

THE REV. NORTON HILL (1826-1895) + CAROLINE WHITE (1832-1922)

**Thomas Rowland** (1851-1936) + Annie McRobert

**Joseph** (1853-1947) + Annie Storrie (1858-1936)

**Mary Jane** (1855-1926) + Hugh Taylor | E. Winter (adopted)

**Norton Blake** (1857-1895) + Mary Rebecca Cody

**Lucy** (1862-1927)

**Randolph James Staples** (1864-1943) + Emeline Farmer (1873-1943)

Leonard + Jessie Glossop | Caroline + Frank Dunlop | Belva (1887-1982) | Gordon (1894-1947) + Marion Higgins
1) Helen (d. 1981)  2) John (d. 1992)   1) Nora Christie  2) Marion (Bobbie), 3) Kerry

Ewart Benjamin Cody (1886-1896) | Henry Norton (1889-1959) + Mabel Ruth (Hart) Jackson (divorced) | Mary Elizabeth ("Betty") (4 children) | Joseph Pearson (b. 1895) + Isabel McFarland Alter

Alvin (died as an infant) | Willam (died at age 3) | Mary Jane ("Jeannie") (1887-1971) | Hugh Taylor (1890-1975) + Florence Lloyd | Willam James (died at age 23)

Lloyd Taylor (1916) + Zena Humble
1) Gay Selby + Robert Swan (2 children)
2) Joy Anne + William Mootz' (1 son)
3) Hugh Leonard ("Tony") + Linda Crowe (1 son)

Olive Lorraine ("Toots") (1918) + Aage Petersen

Wilva Josephine ("Billie") + Murray Forrest
1) Rebecca, (2 children), 2) Gregory

Alan + Barbara Ball
1) Doug, 2) Paula  3) Cori

Joan + Don MacDonald (divorced) | 1) Erik 2), Tom, 3) Jill

Susan + John Bracken | 1) Christine, 2) Kathy  3) John

John Cedric Blake (1900-1958) + Violet Spiers (d. 1976) | Frederick (1910-1969) + Mildred Skelding | Helen | George Randolph (b. 1911) + 1) Bernice Humbolt | 1) Joseph Randolph  2) Frank Leonard  2) Gertrude Morton  3) Charles,  4) Arthur | Annie Greta (b./d. 1903)

Harold (1925) + Stephanie Mallette | (5 children) | Norman (1930) + Helen Schewell | (5 children) | Belva Jean (1933) + Con Luty | (4 children) | Donald (1935) + Betty Dubois | (4 children)

the highway. He often traded with the people of the First Nations, who had a summer campsite where Tally Ho Inn stands today.

Rev. Hill became Huntsville's first minister; his early services were held in George Hunt's home. In 1870 he helped build a school at Hillside. For more than twenty years church services were held there, until the Hillside Church was built in 1892. Hill was often offered freshly harvested crops as payment for his ministry. He died in 1895, but not before securing a promise from his neighbour, Mr. Emberson, to carry on with the Sunday School and to help with the Hillside Church. Mr. Emberson did so faithfully for forty years.

A memorial window in the church commemorates its builders. Rev. Hill's descendants celebrated the church centennial at Tally Ho Inn in 1992.

*ISA*
*(from a story by Hugh T. Hill)*

*The Hill family tree*

*Going for the mail at Grassmere, circa 1911.*
*Left to right: G.E. Henderson, Edith Murgatroyd, Nell Wooldridge,*
*Mrs. G. Richardson, Lola Tilley, Ida and Sylvia Dilworth.*
– Courtesy Sylvia Hurst-Brown

# THE BALLANTINES OF GRASSMERE

Birch Haven is a landmark boathouse on Penlake's north shore; it was built for the boats of J.M. Bullen. His cottage marks the site of one of the earliest cabins — that of Robert Ballantine.

Robert Ballantine was a joiner and pattern-maker from Kilmarnock, Scotland. In 1870 he arrived at Peninsula Lake from Galt, Ontario. With his wife, Mary, and his son, he built a one-room log cabin on a hundred acres of Crown land.

In 1871 Ballantine built a grist mill using water power from the creek that now bears his name. His payment was frequently a percentage of the grain milled.

In 1872 a second son, John, was born. He is said to be the first child of the early settlers to have been born on the lake.

One of Mary Ballantine's friends was Mrs. Norton Hill of Hillside — a close neighbour when the bay was calm enough to cross with a boat or, in winter, frozen enough to cross on foot. The enmity between their husbands, however, as leaders of the Grassmere and Hillside communities respectively, was well known. Hill was an Irish Methodist and a Liberal, while Ballantine was a Scottish Presbyterian and a Tory.

In 1874 Ballantine opened the Grassmere Post Office. He was assisted by William Green of Grassmere Bay, another recipient of a Crown-land grant. Green walked to Huntsville every two weeks to pick up the leather mailbag. When Rev. Hill established the Hillside Post Office in 1878, the rivalry between the men intensified. Complaints to the postmaster that the post offices were situated too close to each other resulted in the closure of the Hillside Post Office a couple of months later.

Robert Ballantine increased his acreage to three hundred, part in Chaffey Township and part in Sinclair. In 1881 St. Paul's Anglican Church was built at Grassmere on property he had owned.

Although Ballantine had envisioned the development of a thriving Grassmere community, a railroad was routed through Huntsville, making it the centre of commerce. In 1886, with his own mill struggling to survive, Ballantine moved with his wife to work in a grist mill at Port Sydney, where he died six years later. His two sons operated the Grassmere Mill until 1895. The post office served the community under Ballantine management until it was closed in 1957.

*DME*

# THE MEREDITHS

"FREE GRANT LAND IN MUSKOKA," read the ads in British newspapers of the second half of the nineteenth century. In 1860 George Meredith emigrated with his family from Ireland to the harsh conditions of newly opened Muskoka. Through the land-grant system, on December 28, 1877, George Meredith, "yeoman," received lots 17 and 18 in the twelfth concession of Franklin Township.

Life for the Meredith family was difficult, made even more so with the untimely death of his wife, Martha. But George and his sons, Robert and William, undaunted by the poor farming conditions, managed to survive. Many early pioneers were ill-equipped to withstand the subzero winter temperatures and eventually moved out West.

The Merediths' first home was a log cabin. Now only the cornerstones mark the site. The original log smokehouse still stands, although it is well over 125 years old. Its rough stone chimney, white-washed door, and hook used for curing meat are all intact.

In 1876 George Meredith and Rev. Norton Hill became the first trustees of the log schoolhouse built in Hillside. George attended the church services held in the Orange Hall at Cain's Corners, where his son Robert served as steward and treasurer.

In 1888 his son William received lots 20 (parcel 88) and 21 in the twelfth concession by Crown patent, which reserved a road allowance on the shore of the lake. Tragedy struck the family when William was killed in a hunting accident in 1895. William's property extended from Peninsula Lake frontage to either side of the trespass road (South Portage Road). He left the land to his father. When George died in 1906, the entire property went to Robert, a game warden and avid book lover.

In anticipation of the arrival of his bride-to-be from the Old Country, Robert built his dream home. He engaged Muskoka master builder and architect William Proudfoot of Huntsville to design it. The result was a six-bedroom, three-storey house made of fieldstone, crafted by a Scottish stonemason. It was the finest residence around with its Palladian window, interior pine panelling, and walnut balustrade, everything he could have wished for his bride. Sadly for Robert, she never arrived.

In 1911 Robert sold just over an acre to Lewis Day Brown for $400. The Brown sisters, Margaret and Helen, often strolled to the Meredith farmstead and picnicked in Orchard Field. In 1921 Robert transferred about half an acre to Wyburn Eastmure for $350.

Robert died, still a bachelor in 1922. The farm was bequeathed to Tom Shaw, who had worked there since the age of twelve. Robert, William, and George Meredith are all buried at the cemetery adjoining St. Paul's Anglican Church in Grassmere.

*George Meredith, circa 1900*
– Courtesy Mrs. Norman Moffat

Tom Shaw sold the farmhouse and property to Robert Burns. The Burns family lived there until 1945, then sold the farmstead to Gordon Hill of Limberlost. It served as a hunt camp for a time; later, Limberlost horses were stabled on the property.

In 1966 Robert Meredith's former holdings were purchased by Norman and Margaret Moffat. As the property was in great disrepair, they undertook the arduous task of restoring it to its former beauty.

*MEM*

## TOM SHAW'S FARM

Thomas McKeown Shaw (1878-1959) was descended from a different sort of pioneer — one of his relatives laid out the first waterworks in Toronto. When Tom was twelve, his father died. His death scattered the seven Shaw children. Tom went north to Muskoka to work on the Meredith farmstead near Hillside.

Tom worked there for many years until wanderlust caused him to seek his fortune out West. He was a patient briefly in the Edam Hospital in Saskatchewan, and while there he fell in love with and married his nurse, Elizabeth "Bessie" Violet Isabelle Burgess. Originally from Hanover, Ontario, Bessie had trained at the Royal Alexandra Hospital in Fergus, graduating in 1914.

When Shaw wrote Bobby Meredith to tell him of his good fortune in finding Bessie — the only fortune he had found out West — Meredith urged him to come home. When Tom, Bessie, and their eighteen-month-old daughter, Maureen, returned to Muskoka, Bobby presented the couple with a "quarter section of land" overlooking the lake. A barn already stood in one field, as it does today, and the land was fertile. The view was wonderful. When Robert Meredith died with no heirs, Tom, who had truly been a son to him, inherited all the Meredith lands.

In the early 1920s Tom's sister, Leah Blackwell, built a cottage just below the farmhouse. Everyone called it the Cottage below the Hill. Farther along the shore another sister, Molly Reddie, built a cottage she named Cozy Nook.

Les Ackerman was a Barnardo boy* who came to live with the Tom Shaw family at the age of nine. In his years on the farm, the Shaw girls, Maureen and Jeanette, thought of him as a brother. Les now lives in Dundas, Ontario.

A distinguished-looking, well-spoken man with permanent laugh wrinkles, Les fondly remembers his life at Penlake, including the time when the big barn was put behind the Shaw farmhouse. "It was moved there," he says, recalling that the barn originally stood where Alexander Fraser had built his house in the 1870s. "Tom's barn was Fraser's barn, rebuilt piece by piece up on the farm."

He recalls the night, when he was fourteen, that Mrs. Shaw gave birth to her second child, Jeanette. "Jim Wright and I hitched up the Democrat, a wagon with a team of two horses, and went to fetch the doctor in the middle of the night. The ground was softening up after the long winter and the road was filled with great ruts." Les rode to the Hill Farm — later called Wonderview Farm —

*Shadowrock Farm*
– Courtesy Mrs. Norman Moffat

*English social reformer Thomas John Barnardo (1845-1905) set in motion a well-intentioned, large-scale program to help destitute children. From about 1870 to 1930 more than 100,000 English children were sent to Canada and arrangements made for them to work as "homeboys" or "homegirls" on farms. Sadly, not all of these arrangements were as successful as Les Ackerman's.*

*The Shaw family. Left to right:*
*Maureen, Jeanette, Tom (back),*
*Les Ackerman and Bessie Shaw.*
– Courtesy Jeanette Shaw Demydas

where there was a phone. He learned from Nettie Lehman, the switchboard operator, that the doctor was stuck about five miles down the road, the running board of his car mired in mud. Les managed to get to the doctor, who abandoned his car and returned to the farm to deliver the infant.

Les remembers sad times as well. He recalls the day when the cattle were first let out of the barn at winter's end. Spurred on by the smell of spring, they raced across the back field toward the bay near the present-day Eastmure cottage. There they encountered melting spring ice — with disastrous results. Les raced back to the barn for one of the draft horses, but was unable to haul the unfortunate beasts from the lake.

Maureen Shaw Hammond and Jeanette Shaw Demydas eagerly share their girlhood memories of the farm: "We walked to the school at Hillside," says Jeanette, "sometimes using the road out from the farm or, when there was ice on the lake, we'd walk right across Hill's Bay. Sometimes we skied to school. Our closest neighbours were at Hillside or North Portage. In harsh winters, there were times when even the horses couldn't get through."

"We wore ski suits to school," remembers Maureen. "We had one big potbellied stove to heat the whole school."

Her sister adds, "Archie Wensley was a good teacher. He taught all nine grades."

The sisters' memories of the homestead are fond. "I was twelve when they put electricity into the farm," says Jeanette. "It cost $50." So proud of having electricity, she spent hours just turning lights on and off!

They recall the root house their father dug near the big barn. There they stored cabbage, turnips, onions, parsnips, pumpkins, squash, beets, carrots, and potatoes. "I remember when Daddy brought home a barrel of apples by horse and wagon. Later we got a jeep. Daddy was blind in one eye and had never driven, so Mother wouldn't drive with him!" (As a teenager Tom Shaw had lost the sight of one eye when lightning struck the Meredith farmhouse.)

Shaw used the jeep for plowing, a step up from the horse-drawn plow he always used. The horses also pulled a stoneboat — a sled that hauled large objects about the farm. During peak vegetable season, Tom loaded his boat by the side of the lake and delivered fresh farm goods to cottage docks. Many cottagers preferred to come to the farm, mooring their boats behind Spurr's dock or at the beach. They would walk up the field to fetch baskets full of fresh, wonderful vegetables.

"One day," muses Maureen, "a big man came to the farm and it was a glorious day. The steamboat *Algonquin* came into view from behind the island and he said, 'Oh, Mrs. Shaw, what a wonderful view!' That was the day our mother named the farm Wonderview Farm!"

Jeanette recalls getting a phone in the 1920s. "There was one wire running through the bush. Mr. Jim Walker, who lived near Bella Lake, took care of that line. If there was trouble, he'd have to walk the entire line through the bush. If a tree was down on the line, God help him! Our ring was a short and a long. There were about twenty-five people on the line. Nettie Lehman was 'central.' We'd pick up and listen, press down, ring the bell, and she'd come on saying, 'Central!' We'd say, 'Hello, Nettie. Would you mind ringing so-and-so?'"

After their daughters married, Tom and Bessie Shaw continued to live on the farm. Much of Tom's inheritance from Robert Meredith had been lost in the early 1920s when a con artist named MacArthur came to town. The man rented the Johnstone cottage by the lake and convinced many local residents that he was a wealthy entrepreneur. Tom Shaw was one of his victims. MacArthur said he planned to turn the Shaw farm into an eighteen-hole golf course. At one time, among the wildflowers and white pines, the putting greens the trusting farmer carved out could be found. By the time MacArthur was finally run out of town, a good number of people had lost their life savings.

In 1947 the Blackwell and Reddie properties were sold to their neighbour, Clint Spurr. Meanwhile, Lang Moffat bought Tom Shaw's farm, as well as Leonard Hill's farm on Highway 60. Lang called his combined holdings Wonderview Farms. He made extensive renovations to the old Hill house, and he and his wife, Marjorie, made it their permanent residence.

Tom and Bessie Shaw moved to a brand-new house near Huntsville where Bessie's beautiful flowers bedecked the land like jewels. Tom died in 1959, Bessie in 1966, but they are far from forgotten. Their small farmhouse, though beyond hope of repair, still stands in silence in the shadow of the big barn. Jeanette Shaw Demydas reflects, "I stand in the silence, but I can still hear the laughter in that little house."

*ISA*

*The Stoneboat: Used for heavy hauling, this early farm conveyance was made of wood with stones incorporated into the bottom to act as skids.*
– Courtesy the Musselman family

# VERNE OKE

VERNE OKE is a carpenter by trade. His property on Grassmere Bay was once the site of E.S. Brooks's lumber mill and is reached by a road east of the Anglican church. Mr. Oke has lived there for thirty-five years in a very comfortable year-round home.

Early in his career he worked at Limberlost Lodge for Gordon Hill, who also owned Tally Ho Inn. Then Hill sent Oke to work for Agnes Kearn and Clare Rose, who managed Tally Ho. He also worked at Pow Wow Point with Bill and Ted West, and Bill Steele when the main building was raised to lay a foundation underneath. He continued to work at Tally Ho with Ted West when the Emberson sisters bought the inn.

*Early logging,
possibly on Ennest Farm.*
– Dilworth photo, courtesy
of VanDuzer

Verne recalls that, in the early days, Bob Constable brought guests to Limberlost from Huntsville by horse and sleigh. A stagecoach operated from Huntsville to Dwight. From there another coach travelled to Dorset.

He spent many winters in the bush cutting timber. In the spring the logs were transported by water to sawmills, usually in Huntsville. Because hardwood logs sink in three days, they had to be raised onto rafts to keep them out of the water. Many such logs ended up at the bottom of Penlake. Although cottager Doug Woollings salvaged many, it was not economically worthwhile. To transport the logs from Penlake to Huntsville, rafts again had to be used because of the restricted dimensions of the canal. By contrast, logs from Vernon Lake were towed to Huntsville in booms by the tugboat *Phoenix*.

Verne Oke also ran a grocery store at the intersection of Highway 60 and the old Highway 11.

His wife was related to the Morgans, who built St. Paul's Anglican Church in Huntsville. Two Morgan families lived at Grassmere: one had property on the way to Pow Wow; the other was up the hill where Hidden Valley is now. Billy Morgan had a farm on the canal. He used a steamboat, moored at the mouth of the canal, to supply the cottagers with vegetables six days a week.

*AMD*

*(from a 1988 interview with Verne Oke when he was eighty-one years old)*

# FRANK WINTERBOTTOM

FRANK WINTERBOTTOM (1899-1970) was a resident of South Portage for sixty-three years. His name became a household word for many Penlake cottagers. Frank was their friend and helper, gifted with an innate understanding of the land and capable beyond words.

Like Les Ackerman, Frank was a Barnardo boy. Born in London, England, one of five children, he came to South Portage when he was eight, and lived with and worked for the Murray family.

At sixteen, Frank struck out on his own, finding jobs in a number of local logging camps. He also worked on the boats that plied Lake of Bays. That was how he met Ella Simmons, his future wife. In 1921 she'd emigrated from England to Toronto; she'd come north to work at the newly opened Bigwin Inn on Lake of Bays — a regular stop for all the big boats.

"Mum and Dad lived in downtown South Portage," says their youngest son, Colin Winterbottom. A small but thriving settlement, South Portage told time by the coming and going of the *Portage Flyer,* affectionately known as the Little Train. Frank was hired as its number-two engineer, a job he held for a number of years.

With three growing sons, Frank, Jack, and Lloyd, and a baby, Colin, on the way, Frank purchased property on South Portage Road. In 1937 he built the house in which Colin lives today. There he tended a vegetable garden and taught his sons to hunt. A nephew, David Wilks, also joined the family as a young teenager.

*Frank Winterbottom refinishing a canoe at the Spurrs' in 1951.*
– Photo by Dibbie Spurr Appleton

While working on the railroad, Frank met the Eastmure family. In 1936 they engaged him to build their cottage in Wolf Bay on Penlake. Over the years, many other cottagers sought out Frank and his wife, Ella, as trusted helpers. Ella was known for planting a garden so that it would be blooming by the time the cottager arrived in the spring. She also swept away the cobwebs and winter dirt, and did the washing for many of the cottagers. Ella was known for her exquisite quilts. I have two quilts of hers that I treasure, and I marvel at the delicate hand-stitching.

Joan Eastmure Pratt remembers that when she was a child, "Frank walked over the mountain late in the evening after a day of work on the train to lay our flagstone paths. We were supposed to be asleep, but we'd watch Frank at work, and he'd make us laugh by making faces at us while he worked."

Frank Winterbottom was loved by young and old. He didn't talk much about himself. A modest man, he was gentle, giving, and kind. Laugh lines creased his suntanned face. Frank died in the spring of 1970.

*ISA*

# MARTIN IVERSON

In the early 1900s Martin Iverson, a Norwegian baker, became a permanent resident at North Portage. He had a wife, three young daughters, and an infant son.

He kept a few cattle and cut a crop of hay each year from his hay field, which ran from the Portage toward White Rock Mountain. He also farmed another piece of land just off the Canal Road about a mile from his house. When my family was up there on holidays, my dad often gave Martin a hand with the haying, pitching the haycocks up onto the wagon. When no more could be loaded, my brother and I rode on the top all the way to the barn — a great thrill for city kids!

To supplement his income, Martin worked as a cook in the lumber camps during the winters. He eventually became a cook at the new summer resort Limberlost Lodge, which is where we first met him. He interested my dad in buying a lot from him on the water in Wolf Bay. At this time he had already sold lots to both Rev. Marshall and Tom Taylor. When we bought ours in 1921, we got it for a dollar a foot.

*The view from the Penlake Post Office in 1946.*
– Courtesy Don Marshall

Martin was to build us a log cabin by the following summer. When we arrived via the *Algonquin* on the first of July, we found not a log cabin, but a frame house with four walls ten feet high, four narrow windows, a solid front door, and a very steep roof (so the snow would slide off). This was not our dream cabin by any means, but Martin had cooked in a camp all winter and hadn't had time to retrieve logs to build our cabin. In 1931 it became the first cottage in Wolf Bay to get hydro. The frame house lasted in a patched-up fashion until we tore it down in 1960 and built another.

One night in the summer of 1923 Martin Iverson raced from cottage to cottage, banging on the doors and shouting, "Come help Wawa! She burn down!" It seemed the prestigious Wawa Hotel, built on Lake of Bays in 1908 by the Canadian Railway News Company, was on fire. The cottagers worked all night at North Portage transferring the victims to the steamboats *Algonquin* and *Ramona* from the Little Train, and sending them on to the hospital. The train and boats ran all night long and most of the next day. Eight Wawa staff members perished in the blaze.

The Iverson farm was quite neglected, but a few years later Martin built himself a bake shop near his house. A square dance was held in it for the grand opening. He became famous for his bread and pies, selling many to Bigwin Inn.

His bake shop contained two long wooden troughs with loose wooden covers where he put the dough to rise. He told us children that in busy times he would sleep on top of these troughs. When the dough rose, it tilted the wooden covers and rolled him onto the floor. That meant it was time to bake the loaves. We believed him!

His business declined as roads improved and people were able to travel farther to shop. One winter the frost heaved the store chimney, parting it from the bake shop and leaving the ovens useless. Martin moved his family to South River, where he opened another bake shop. He operated this shop successfully until his death in the late 1960s.

During these early years, Mr. Benedict, the one-armed Indian, and his daughter, Adele, set up a tent amongst the trees in front of Portage Lodge. Every day except Sunday, Mr. Benedict would take a huge basket filled with assorted small baskets and Indian wares up to Bigwin Inn to sell to the guests. The basket would invariably come back empty. Adele was a trained nurse, but she loved to spend the summers camping with her dad. We used to visit Adele in the tent, and she taught us how to make bookmarks from sweet grass.

*JMS*

# SYD BULLOCK

*Syd and Albert Bullock, photo taken in England prior to leaving for Canada, circa 1914.*
— Courtesy Roy Bullock

SYD BULLOCK was born in the Guernsey Islands. In 1914, when he was seven, he and his brother, Albert, came to Canada as Barnardo boys. They were brought to Penlake from Huntsville in the Blackburn launch, and disembarked at the government dock in Hillside — today called Maplehurst Drive — where their foster family picked them up.

As was the case with many home boys, Syd and Albert were not well treated. Consequently they were transferred to another family in Dwight, one that already had forty-five Barnardo boys! After that, Syd moved to South Portage.

For many years he worked with Bob Wright. When Syd got married, he went out on his own. His jobs were numerous and varied, and they included working on Highway 60 and the Algonquin Park Road, then on the steamboat *Iroquois* and at Brook's Mill. He was also hired for a time by Billy Ennest, a local farmer.

In 1942 Syd bought his own house. Located just behind the old North Portage store, it had originally been the Iverson Bakery. Syd also bought 114 acres of land, including a thousand feet of shoreline in Wolf Bay, for $3,000. In addition, he purchased the property between the old Portage Lodge and Dr. Ross's cottage, and owned the large brick house at Cain's Corner, originally owned by the Blackwell family. After amassing all this property, Syd proceeded to sell it, piece by piece.

Norm and Margaret Moffat bought some of the Wolf Bay property and Jim Shipton bought the property near Portage Lodge.

For a short while Syd was hired to do renovations on the old Portage Lodge. John Turner had purchased the place in the early 1970s with the intention of converting it into a disco. During the renovation process Syd found old newspapers fastened to the walls. Used as insulation, these were 1893 and 1894 issues of the *Montreal Star* and the *Toronto Mail*. Although yellowed and brittle with age, they are still legible. Syd Bullock died in the summer of 1993.

*RDM*

# THE BOB WRIGHT FAMILY

THE WRIGHT FAMILY was an institution on the Springsyde shore. Bob and "Ma" Wright had six children: Lorne, Jim, St. Clair, Sam, List, and Pearl.

Bob came to Canada from England in the early 1900s and settled at Udney near Orillia. Lorne, the eldest child, was born there. Shortly after, the Wrights moved to South Portage and then to Springsyde, where Bob bought a small farm behind the Hall cottage. Fire destroyed the farmhouse just after it had been painted. He rebuilt and lived there until he sold it to Alex Thompson in 1937. Today it is almost impossible to see where the old house once stood, and there is no trace of the outbuildings.

Although Bob worked at just about everything along the shore, he really didn't like to work. He preferred to think of himself as a fish guide and availed himself of every opportunity to be just that on Penlake and Lake of Bays.

Bob built most of the boathouses along the Springsyde shore, and each had a cluster of pilings, or spiles, in front for protection from the ice. Bob would build a spile-driving tower, which he would set up on the ice. Through a series of pulley arrangements, his team of horses hauled the heavy maple spiling hammer to the top of the tower, where one of his sons would be perched, ready to trip the hammer. This process would be repeated again and again until all the spiles had been driven home.

After a heavy snowfall Bob's team of horses would haul the spiling hammer along the Springsyde path to clear a way for his children to walk to school. After reaching North Portage, it was only another mile to the school at South Portage.

On a Saturday evening the Wright farmhouse would be bouncing with square dancers. Bob would levy a small charge, Syd Bullock would usually play the fiddle, and Bob's son Lorne would do the calling. He was, in fact, a favourite caller on the square-dancing circuit, including the dances at Joe Bullen's across the lake and at the golf club pavilion.

*Bob Wright and his children Lorne, Jimmy, and Pearl.*
– Courtesy Irwin Schultz

Ma Wright, who'd been baking since she was fourteen, provided the Springsyde cottagers with some of the best baked goods to be found in the area. Her special buns, painted with syrup and sprinkled with sugar, were an absolute delight. Besides the baked goods, the Wrights supplied cottagers with milk from their four cows and vegetables from their garden.

Lorne Wright loved to enter the solo canoe race at the regatta. As he powered his canoe through the water like a huge battleship, he was a sight to behold. No one could beat him — until the year that fifteen-year-old Ian Eastmure, using the family racing canoe and exercising great finesse, bested Lorne by several boat-lengths.

It was sad to see the Wrights leave the shore, though Sam continued on the lake for many years, working for the McCreadys at the golf course, as well as at their cottage and home in Pittsburgh. St. Clair worked for Erik Skat-Petersen awhile before and after the Second World War, and then started his own taxi business in Huntsville. Lorne, Sam, and St. Clair have all passed away now, and Jim is living in a retirement home just outside Huntsville. Pearl and List have established homes beyond the Huntsville area.

*RDM*

# JOHN ALEXANDER THOMPSON

IN THE EARLY 1930S MY FATHER, Alex Thompson, began working at Springsyde. Our home was in South Portage. My cousin Charlie Peterson — who later became Dad's right-hand man — remembers how, at the age of eleven, he helped Dad deliver milk and vegetables. Dad kept a rowboat padlocked to a tree on Walker's Beach and rowed from North Portage to beyond Put-in-Bay with his deliveries. F.W. Moffat (Frederick William) at Corralyn was among the first of the summer residents for whom my father worked.

*Alex and Alice Thompson, circa 1960.*
– Courtesy Dorothy Thompson Newman

In 1937 we bought the Bob Wright farm. As time passed, Dad's workload included more and more customers from Put-in-Bay to Wolf Bay. He became caretaker for twenty-six Springsyde cottages. Eventually he had to hire more men. He spent many Saturdays collecting his accounts and establishing what jobs needed to be done.

There are many monuments to Dad's skill on Peninsula Lake, including stonework at F.W. Moffat's, Musselman's, and Dilworth's. He and Charlie Peterson built roads from the township road into the Lucas, Mansell, and Cameron cottages, among others.

In 1945 we purchased the bungalow store and property from the Waltons. My mother became postmistress, and we worked as a family in the store and tearoom. We sold the store in 1948 to Mr. and Mrs. Samuel Manning. Dad then bought the house beside the Portage Lodge from Charlie.

After leaving this property, my parents bought a home on Brunel Road in Huntsville. In 1964 they bought a cottage on Lake of Bays. Dad still worked along the Springsyde shore until 1966 or 1967, when Carl Thompson took over the caretaking.

My dad passed away, suddenly, of a heart attack on May 12, 1972. My husband, Bob, and I bought the Lake of Bays property from my mother in 1976 and retired here in 1980.

*Dorothy Thompson Newman*

# ERIK SKAT-PETERSEN

ORIGINALLY FROM DENMARK, ERIK PETERSEN, his wife, Margaret, his daughter, Helga, and his two sons, Aage and Knud, came to Penlake in the 1930s. Eric and his sons had been commissioned to build a cottage for J.M. Bullen, which is now the Potters' cottage near Pow Wow. The Petersen men went on to construct many summer homes around the lake, including the Weaber, Foster, Dalton, Spurr, and Norman Moffat cottages. They also built other structures in the region, including the entrance gates at Algonquin Park and the park museum.

When the Petersens built the Foster cottage, Hie Away, in 1937, Eleanor Foster worked closely with Erik Petersen, but apparently not closely enough! When she and her husband, George, arrived to see the finished product, they found carvings of squirrels at every roof tip, owls and squirrels over every doorway and window inside and out, and dragons festooning the ends of every eave. She mentioned to Mr. Petersen that there were perhaps too many animals, but he just shrugged and said that was the way he did things. The master builder was not going to take orders from a mere five-foot-two American lady who spoke no Danish.

Eleanor implored George to tell the man to get rid of the wildlife, or at least most of it. Mildly enjoying her discomfort, George said he wouldn't consider insulting a man of such consummate skill. It would be like one of his patients telling him how to stitch an incision.

Biding her time, Eleanor finally had the chance to speak with Mr. Petersen privately. She said quietly, with just a hint of staged embarrassment, that some-times Dr. Foster had a drinking problem. When he'd been drinking, she said, he sometimes liked to shoot animals, especially owls. Therefore, what with the near impossibility of getting Dr. Foster to give up drink, surely Mr. Petersen could understand that having those carvings over every doorway and window presented a grave danger to her and the children. The builder apparently allowed that some men did indeed have drinking problems, so down came two dozen owls, twice as many squirrels, and six dragons.

A skilled cabinetmaker, he also made much of the furniture in the Foster cottage, including the dining-room table, buffet and chairs, and a beautiful drop-front desk, which sits underneath the charming spiral staircase in the living room.

In Erik Petersen's later years — he lived into his nineties — his hobby was making various small wooden articles. He was especially known for his small, colourfully painted, four-legged stools, cherished by many cottagers. For his own outhouse, he made two seat covers, one called Tragedy and the other Comedy. His daughter, Helga, regrets that they were eventually sold to an American tourist.

*Briar Foster and AMD*

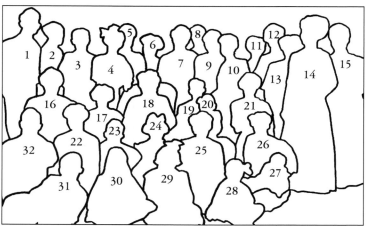

*Ogle Anniversary Party – pre-First World War:*

*1. G.E. Henderson, 2. Mrs. W. Marshall, 3. Will Marshall,*
*4. Jean Millar (McEwen), 5. Isabel Millar, 6. ?,*
*7. Helen (Nellie) P. Brown, 8. ?, 9. ?, 10. Mrs. Elmsley,*
*11. Mary McLean, 12. Margaret Miner, 13. Fannie Richardson,*
*14. ?, 15. Elizabeth Day Whitman, 16. ?, 17. Helen Brown (Cook),*
*18. Mrs. Ogle, 19. Mr. Ogle, 20. Florence Richardson,*
*21. Nell Wooldridge, 22. Barbara Luscious, 23. Toge Ogle,*
*24. Mildred Ogle, 25. Vi Ogle, 26. Ida Dilworth,*
*27. Roz Dilworth (baby), 28. Sylvia Dilworth, 29. Lillian Andrews,*
*30. ?, 31. Roy Henderson, 32. Lewis Day Brown, Jr.*

– Courtesy Ted Harper

# The Coming of the Cottagers

## EARLY YEARS ON PENINSULA LAKE

WHEN entry into Peninsula Lake became easier around the turn of the century, cottagers began to settle along the shores. At the time the pioneer land grants extended to the edge of the lake.

### Pym's Point

TWO of the earliest cottagers were Mr. and Mrs. Edward Pym from Huntsville. According to the 1890 *Huntsville Forester*, they established a summer cottage "in the shade and away from the summer heat" on what is now called Pym's Point. This was likely a shore lot from the land granted to Casselman.

### Inkerman

THE NAME INKERMAN on the boathouse identified the original Grant summer residence on Penlake. Donald McKenzie Grant, KC, and his wife, Marguerite, purchased the land from Casselman in 1908 for $100. The summer cottage was erected shortly thereafter.

Like the Pyms, the Grants were Huntsville residents. Donald, a member of the first graduating class of Osgoode Hall, was Huntsville's first resident lawyer. With no road to their cottage, however, he boated to and from his Huntsville law office daily in a single-piston inboard.

The First World War shattered the Grant family's idyllic summer routine. Donald had a developing military career with the Simcoe Foresters. When war broke out, he was commissioned to raise a battalion from the districts of Muskoka and Parry Sound to go overseas. He formed the 122d Battalion and led it to England in 1917.

After Marguerite died in 1946, the family no longer used the cottage and it fell into disrepair. When the Gillers purchased it in 1955, time had left its mark, but they found mementoes of the war stored in the attic: gas masks, large German shell casings, Donald Grant's rifle box, and a German helmet.

*William J. Giller*

*The Inkerman cottage, circa 1910. Note the two verandahs.*
– Courtesy Bill Giller

THE ISLAND in the centre of Peninsula Lake has had a long history of ownership and resulting name changes. Called Isle Donnel in the mid-1800s when it was discovered by the two surveyors, it became Hill's Island in 1867, when Rev. Norton Hill received a Crown grant to the property. Twenty-four years later he sold it for $200 to William Wesley Walker, then serving the Hillside congregation prior to his ordination in 1891, and so the island became known as Walker's Island. In 1901 Rev. Walker sold it to his sister-in-law, Julia Shearer, for $1000. In 1903 she sold it for $1950 to Gideon Eugene "Gene" Henderson, Dr. George G. Richardson, and Robert James Berkinshaw. The island was not subdivided at this time, but each of the three owners built a cottage. In 1911 Mr. Berkinshaw sold his one-third interest to Gene Henderson for $2300.

In September of the same year, the island, now known as Dunelg, but to this day often referred to as Hill's Island, was formally divided into three parts, with Dr. Richardson obtaining the deed to the northern one, Gene Henderson the central one, and Edmund A. Ogle the southern one (purchased from Gene Henderson). Each agreed to erect no more than a single dwelling on his parcel of land.

*The Henderson boat at locks in 1918. Henderson (in cap) with L.D. Brown family, on an outing. Approximately 30 feet long, this launch was fast, powered by a huge six-cylinder Sterling engine.*
– Courtesy the Spurr family

Alfred Harper, who used to visit the island in the summer, was a friend and schoolmate of the Henderson boys — Roy, Fred, and Rex. Alfred met, courted and on August 4, 1919, married Mildred Ogle in St. Paul's Anglican Church at Grassmere. In honour of his daughter's wedding, Edmund Ogle had the frame church clad in red brick. This gift is commemorated on a plaque inside the church.

Following the death of her husband, Fanny Richardson sold the northern portion of the island and its cottage to her brother, William Marshall, in 1919. William and his wife, Mae, used to stay with their five children at Deerhurst and visit the Richardsons. Upon obtaining the cottage, they began to take their family there, instead, along with two maids and a groundsman.

Gene Henderson's large cottage (which still stands) in the centre of the island actually encompassed one of the original Walker cabins. A spacious dining room was added to the southwest of the original room, with a fireplace at the far end and good-size windows with seats. The wraparound verandah was complete with an old swinging couch, and from it wide steps led down the path to the front dock where the steamboat *Algonquin* used to stop.

## Wolf Island

"NINE-TENTHS OF AN ACRE, more or less," reads the original grant. Wolf Island and its companion, Cubby Island, are included in one of the lake's earliest Crown grants. In May 1893 the two parcels were issued to George Simpson, a journalist from Chicago, Illinois, later of Huntsville. In 1905 George and his sons built a stone house on the larger island but there is evidence that the old stone-and-timber house that stands on the site today may not be the original cottage.

In 1907 the Simpsons transferred the property to W.G.A. Millar from Pittsburgh — Walt and Isobel Millar were close friends who used to rent a cottage at Fisher's Point — and George Elmslie from Chicago.

Walt Millar was actively involved in the formation of the North Muskoka Lakes Association (NMLA). It was his idea that a yearbook of the association be printed in 1938, and he served as chairman of the committee. But that very year there was a most unfortunate event. This insertion appeared in the NMLA Year Book, 1938-39:

> Mr. Millar's death is tragic. Homeward bound from Huntsville on Wednesday night, July 27th, in the company of Mrs. Millar and Miss Ila Oke of Huntsville, his car left the road beyond Hillside and upset. W.G.A. Millar died shortly after the accident.

Wolf and Cubby islands eventually passed into the hands of Walt's daughter, Jean Primrose Millar, who married Frederick Bates McEwen of Pittsburgh. She also inherited George Elmslie's share of the property, and at her death, the islands were inherited by her children — Malcolm, Bill, and Sandy.

*A 1918 view from Wolf Mountain.*
– Photo by Margaret Brown, courtesy Spurr family

## Put-in-Bay

DID THIS DELIGHTFUL LITTLE BAY get its name because of the four original cottages being put in the bay, or does the name have some symbolic reference to the battle of Put-in-Bay during the War of 1812? No one can say. But Mrs. Grace Blackburn, who built the cottages in 1902, was a romantic as well as an astute businesswoman. She named two of the cottages after her favourite English novels *East Lynn* and *Anne Marie*.

Grace's cottages were rented out every summer. As there was no road, the tenants were brought by boat from Huntsville, either in the motor launch Grace's husband, William Charles Blackburn, built (aptly named *Put-in-Bay*), or in the steamers *Ramona* and *Algonquin*. On a clear day the remains of the crib where the dock was built for the steamers can still be seen.

In 1942, just before her death, Grace sold her Put-in-Bay property to Leona Newton and her brother, Bob Terry. Over the years, the Put-in-Bay cottages fell into disrepair, and two were torn down.

## Springsyde

THE SHORE KNOWN AS SPRINGSYDE is a series of subdivisions devised over a number of years. The first plan was not registered. The second plan, Springbank, was registered in June 1903. The third was named West Springbank and was registered in 1908. Next came East Springbank in 1910.

*Put-in-Bay*
– Courtesy Irwin Schultz

*Minutes of an early*
**Springbank Association meeting.**
– Courtesy Springsyde
Association Archives

***Springsyde Shore - pre-1926 postcard***
– Courtesy Irwin Schultz

East of this, the shore remained undivided for thirty-one years, and the terrain through the birch trees along the shore to the railway crossing at the Portage became a favourite walk for all the cottagers. Judy (Purdy) Maunder recalled that, as a teenager, she used the path so frequently that she could easily walk along it at night without a flashlight; she knew every stone and tree around which the path curved! In 1941 the land was divided into shore lots.

The Springbank Cottagers' Association began in 1905, when eleven cottagers met, including Professor Albert Laing, William Mansell, and J.K. (John King), T.L. (Thomas Lang) and F.W. (Frederick William) Moffat.

In 1909 mail service to the area, which was as yet inaccessible by road, began. The *Algonquin* would drop off a mailbag and pick up outgoing mail at Springbank Wharf. However, by 1910 it became clear that the Penlake address was being confused with the Springbank Post Office near London, Ontario. The association decided to form a committee to find a new name and to begin incorporation procedures. At an association meeting on August 23, 1912, the membership approved a report presented by the committee that read: "The Place [is] to be known as Springsyde and the association [is] to be known as Springsyde Cottagers' Association as set forth in the charter, constitution and by-laws of the incorporation."

## *Winoka Shore*

ALL THE LOTS, from the golf course up to and including the entire Winoka property, were part of:

> The Plan of Idlewyld Summer Resort, being a subdivision of part of lots 24 and 25 Concession XIV, Township of Franklin, the property of Miss Lucy E. Hill and Randolph J.S. Hill from the will of the Rev. Robert Norton Hill deceased. Dated January 1904, Huntsville, Ontario.

The Rev. A.B. Winchester and his brother, Judge John Winchester, bought two large lots from Lucy Hill in 1904 and built cottages the following year.

From 1905 to 1910 Lucy Hill built several cottages along the shore. They were purchased by Professor Angus and later sold to various people, including Ernest Crabtree and Mr. and Mrs. Rea.

In 1914 John Bridges sold a large acreage of the Grassmere Peninsula to Judge John Winchester of Winoka. Upon his death, Mrs. Winchester and the Winchester estate sold the timber rights for $1500 to John G. Golden, who carried on a lumber business in Huntsville and owned a mill in Grassmere Bay. The J. Howard Winchester cottage on the shore of the bay dates from Judge Winchester's purchase, as do the properties now owned by Gracia Potter and Bea Gordon, granddaughters of the judge.

*Three philosophers, 1918: Professor Angus, A.B. Winchester, and Professor Laing.*
– Courtesy David W. Gordon

*A 1912 view of the Winoka dock taken from aboard the S.S.* Algonquin.
– Courtesy Mary Winchester Jack and David Winchester Gordon

## Portage to Flat Rock

The area from Portage to Flat Rock was first settled in 1908. J.S. Barker's summer home was begun that year, and it was mostly completed by 1910. The little compound consisted of a main house, servants' house, powerhouse, icehouse, boathouse, and garage. Auto travel to the lake was quite an excursion in those days. Cars had much smaller horsepower, and in some places the roads were little more than ruts. With the weather, one never knew what to expect. If it had been raining, good luck! This was an all-day journey.

The Rev. David Heggie Marshall, at the time the minister of St. Andrew's Presbyterian Church in Huntsville, also built his cottage in 1908. A tax bill from 1921 requests payment of two dollars or to "work one day on the roads." Rev. Marshall chose to work.

Mr. Fisher built three cottages on the point, which was named after him. These he rented. In 1911 Rev. Marshall encouraged Tom Taylor to build a cottage, and Wee Neuke is still enjoyed by his daughter, Mary Hutchinson, and her family. David Marshall and Tom Taylor used to take turns each evening walking over White Rock Mountain — in back of Wolf Bay — to a farm at South Portage for buckets of milk.

In 1921 the Macpherson family had Martin Iverson build them a cottage. Macpherson often gave Iverson a hand with his haying, pitching the haycocks up on the wagon. Jessie Stuart fell heir to this property.

Another early cottage on the bay is that of Mrs. Duncan McIntosh (née Mary McLennan). Her father was one of the ministers on the shore.

### Township of Franklin

Birkendale P.O., Ont., _____ 192_

Mr. _____

Please take notice that there are ___1___ days Statute Labor charged against your property, Lot _P 23_ in Con _12_ in the Township of Franklin for the year 192_ Computed at $2.00 per day, this represents the total sum of _Two_ _____ DOLLARS

($2__) which you are requested to pay direct on or before _____ 192_ to C. J. C. CRUMP, Treasurer, Birkendale P.O., Ont.

## Flat Rock

AT THE EASTERN END OF PENLAKE is an abrupt and significant rise of granite affectionately known as Wolf Mountain. Nestled below this high terrain is Flat Rock, a broad expanse of rock that slopes gently into the water.

Over the years Flat Rock has been the site of numerous picnics and overnight camp-outs. On occasion canoe trippers sought refuge there. One rain-soaked evening in the early 1950s the members of a girls' canoe trip from Minioee did just that. They had missed their train portage from North to South Portage. However, the storm proved too severe and the nearby Moffat boathouse offered more inviting shelter.

A twenty-minute walk on the path up Wolf Mountain is rewarded with a wonderful vista of the lake. From its lofty heights in the midst of a forest, it's easy to imagine earlier days when native peoples camped on the shoreline.

This land, purchased by Margaret and Norman Moffat from Syd Bullock in 1952, was never built upon, and remains one of the few areas of the lake offering an untouched natural landscape.

*Picnic at Flat Rock*
– Courtesy Appleton

## Eastern Shore

IN 1879 THE CROWN SOLD LAND on the eastern shore to Alexander and Ann Fraser. They built a log house with a stone foundation to shelter their family, of at least six children. A large barn was erected as well. A small rise in the field gives a hint of where the house may have stood.

Upon Alexander's death in 1888, one hundred and eighty-six acres of his land went to a son, John. When John moved, he sold his land to a neighbour, Robert Meredith. A small portion of the holdings where Alexander and two other family members were buried was retained. A stone cairn has been erected to mark the site.

Alexander Fraser's daughter, Robena, who married George Johnstone of Toronto, chose to build on the lake. Her property may well have been a part of the original Fraser homestead. The Johnstones were true cottagers, as their presence at the lake was seasonal rather than year-round.

The Johnstone cottage has two storeys, though the second level is only one room. A small log sleeping cabin stands nearby and it has materials from the original Fraser cottage, including square-head nails, common at the turn of the century. A large boathouse once served the cottage, sheltering George Johnstone's much-admired boat, which he himself designed. A highly skilled craftsman, he also designed launches for various cottagers on the lower Muskoka lakes.

For several years the Johnstone cottage was rented. Robena and her daughter, Hildreth, had moved into the smaller log cabin. The walls were lined with pictures of natives, for on her mother's side, Robena was of First Nations' descent. She had wonderful tales to tell, and delighted in the telling. Visits with her had a

*The Johnstone boat and boathouse. George Johnstone built his own boat in 1918.*
– Courtesy the Spurr family

*A train coming in at Huntsville station, circa 1910.*
– Courtesy Don Marshall

*A traffic jam at North Portage. The S.S.* Algonquin *waits for the* Ramona *to depart.*
– Courtesy Don Marshall

*The only known photo of Bob Meredith.*
*Left to right: Margaret Brown (Spurr), Crawf Brown, Bob Meredith, Helen*
*Brown (Cook), Elizabeth Brinkman, Lew Brown, and Ed Fillman, circa 1917.*
– Courtesy the Spurr family

*Wyburn and Gerry Eastmure,*
*circa 1929.*
– Courtesy Joan Eastmure Pratt

mystical quality. Hildreth Johnstone never married, and in 1947 the property was sold to Donald and Isabel McIntosh.

When Mr. and Mrs. Lewis Day Brown decided to build on Peninsula Lake, they searched for a distant undeveloped shore. They met Robert Meredith, who owned a vast stretch of land on the eastern end of the lake. In 1911 they purchased a beautiful piece of this land from him. Located where the lake becomes Wolf Bay, the site was often referred to by early cottagers as Brown's Point. The cottage, which Mrs. Brown called Windstone, was built around 1915 by a man named Walker.

Wyburn "Wy" Eastmure of Toronto first came to Peninsula Lake to visit his army buddy, Freeman "Toge" Ogle. Toge's family owned one of the three cottages on Isle Dunelg. Wy and Toge frequently took canoe trips to Algonquin Park. On one visit, Wy accompanied the Ogles to a party and square dance being hosted by Mrs. Brown at Brown's Point. He told her about his love for the area and she suggested that he speak with Robert Meredith, who owned much of the land behind her cottage, as well as that to the south in Wolf Bay. Wy took her advice and spoke with Meredith the next morning. Wy's daughter, Joan Eastmure Pratt, says, "Dad bought the property then and there for a dollar a foot." The year was 1919.

In the late 1920s Mr. and Mrs. Miller of Pittsburgh built a cottage and boathouse on the shore by Grassy Island. Mrs. Miller lived to be quite old. She and her family vacationed at the cottage for many years. Shortly after her death, her son, Maynard, sold to Lang Moffat, who owned Wonderview Farms behind it. In 1970 Margaret and David Kennard bought the cottage.

Bea Moffat and her husband, Dr. Howard Charlton, built their cottage, Sunset Point, in 1931. Lang Moffat III and his wife, Marjorie, built their cottage, Kialami, in 1934.

A small frame cottage at the foot of Hill's Bay stands on the lot that Rowland Hill reserved for his daughter, Belva (1887-1982). Built in 1951 in the corner of a field, the cottage was named Little Field. For many years Belva's cottage was enveloped by a forest of young trees, which protected it somewhat from the passing cars on Maplehurst Drive and Shaw's Road.

Belva Hill never married. When she died in 1982, her property was to have passed to a niece, Helen Dunlop Johnston. However, Helen predeceased Belva, so the cottage passed instead to Helen's brother, John, who had built his own cottage along Shaw's Road.

**The Historical Committee**

Belva wrote this poem about Little Field cottage:

*I love to walk in woodland green*
*Where tall white birches stand serene,*
*Casting their dappled shadows low*
*On spring-flower carpets' sunny glow.*
*In these I see most every hue,*
*Foam flower white and violets blue,*
*Spring beauties pink and soft with dew.*
*And over yonder by a tree*
*Jack-in-his-Pulpit I chance to see*
*Standing there so straight and bold,*
*Preaching sermons I've been told;*
*Dutchman's breeches snowy white*
*In fringy foliage tucked in tight.*
*And in the evening when 'tis still*
*The thrush with music sweet and shrill*
*The very woodland seems to fill.*
*Then in the bay not far around*
*I hear a thund'rous stirring sound:*
*"Knee deep, knee deep, go 'round, go 'round,"*
*And later still out on the lake*
*A loon calls wildly for his mate.*
*Oh happy days so full of zest,*
*And quiet nights for needed rest!*
*To these small things my thoughts now yield,*
*It's summer-time at Little Field!*

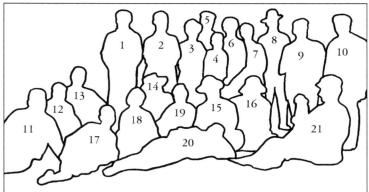

*The gathering from Springsyde and Isle Dunelg:*

*1. Andrew White, 2. P.C. Mansell, 3. Ella Mansell,*
*4. Bill Mansell, 5. Dr. Richardson,*
*6. Florence (Mansell) Morish, 7. Eveline (Hill) Mansell,*
*8. ?, 9. Uncle Harry Mansell, 10. Uncle Dick Mansell,*
*11. Alex Purdy, 12. Alf Harper, 13. Wm. Mansell,*
*14. Edith Murgatroyd, 15. Mrs. Ogle, 16. Vi Ogle,*
*17. Mr. Ogle, 18. Mildred Ogle, 19. Mrs. Richardson,*
*20. Freeman Ogle, 21. Mr. Henderson.*

– Courtesy Dorothy Mansell Eastmure

# TANGLEWOOD

THE FIRST MANSELLS TO ENTER THE REGION were my paternal grandparents, William and Eveline Mansell, who visited friends on what is now Isle Dunelg just before the turn of the century. My grandfather was so impressed by the beach across the lake from the island that he purchased it, along with much of the land behind and alongside it.

The Mansell cottage, Tanglewood, was erected in 1904. It was definitely occupied when the *Portage Flyer* made its first run; my father told me he refused a ride on that occasion because the tracks were not yet ballasted.

Transportation to Tanglewood in those days was by the Grand Trunk Railway to Huntsville. The most popular train left Toronto close to midnight on Friday or in the very early hours of Saturday. Overnight berth accommodation was required because the trip was a lengthy one, made so by backing to, and returning from, Muskoka Wharf at Gravenhurst. The return trip from the wharf was arduous, because the grade almost defeated the steam locomotives.

Frequently, two sections were required on the Friday-night train, with three being the invariable rule on Civic Holiday weekend. On the earlier section, the car for Huntsville would be dropped on a siding; but passengers on later sections would be required to dress and, in the case of men, shave with straight razors, while the train swerved and jerked around the sharp curves north of Bracebridge.

The walk to the waiting steamer was over tracks and cinders, at times blazing hot from the heat of the sun. One had to be watchful as the Huntsville railroad yard was a busy one, with its own turntable and roundhouse, plus a yard engine that puffed about almost all day, usually running the baggage cars down to a siding by the wharf for unloading. Meanwhile, the road engine would go to the water tank for a refill.

Passengers who boarded the steamer at the station dock had to walk through clouds of steam floating up from various vents of the waiting vessel. Mingling with the smothering smell of steam were soft-coal smoke, wood smoke, and the appetizing odour of freshly cut wood and sawdust from the nearby sawmill.

Once the vessel was under way a lunch counter opened, and the usual fare was sandwiches of ham or cheese, doughnuts, pie and tea, coffee or milk.

The purser advised the captain of calls to be made en route. If a cottager wanted the steamer to call at a wharf, a white flag was flown. The captain, of course, might ignore the signal until his return trip, unless there was a good reason to stop.

Crowds stood on the sometimes rickety docks, greeting disembarking passengers with delight and exchanging taunts and good-natured gibes with those remaining on board.

The baggage, from small suitcases to large steamer trunks, was trundled off or on using two-wheeled baggage carts that clunked over the gangplank. They would be under the guidance of the dock-hand; but where transfer was heavy, as it was at North Portage, all members of the crew, including the captain and excepting the engineer, would pitch in. The engineer was exempt, I think, because of his advanced age. At North Portage, where the wait was usually lengthy, he would fish from the stern of the vessel.

A passenger on many trips was an elderly Algonquin who peddled crafts of birchbark, beads, and porcupine quills.

The first view around the wharfs, whether at Springsyde or North Portage, was of pilings vanishing into murky depths. Ears were met with familiar sounds of water lapping on the shore, while the nostrils were assailed by the stench of a moribund sucker.

The steamers, of course, also transported mail and freight. The mail, in a canvas bag, was flung ashore by the purser. Freight was rattled over the gangplank and dumped onto the dock to await the pleasure of the addressee.

Southbound trains were at the mercy of the steamers, so that any undue delay on the lakes meant that a train departed behind schedule. Meetings in the canal of a steamer and a tug towing a boom of logs or a barge of hemlock bark were extremely frustrating. Complaints were heaped on the snail-like progress of such traffic by steamer and private-launch occupants alike.

The popular return train left Huntsville at about 6 p.m., standard time, and so the dining car was a busy spot as the train neared Barrie. Heavy linens graced the tables, as did finger bowls. While accepting the elegant service, one could only marvel at the waiters' dexterity as they carried loaded trays while the train lurched around sharp curves. With daylight saving not yet in vogue, most of the return trip was spent in darkness. The engineer, vainly trying to make up for the time lost at Muskoka Wharf, would hang on to the whistle cord as the train screeched through the blackness of Simcoe and York counties. I have used the train in recent years and have found little difference in travel time.

The walk from Springsyde Wharf to Tanglewood was pleasant, as long as one had no more than a single valise. If one was more heavily burdened, the excess was transported to its destination in a punt, courtesy of the Cottagers' Association. Normally the punt was tied up at the wharf, but on occasion, it broke free and landed near Hillside Bay. I returned it once by towing it behind a canoe, the most laborious trip I've ever made.

The most satisfying welcome, in my mind, was the pungent aroma of cedars clustered about Springsyde Wharf. It told me I was home again. Then there was the aroma I met upon entering our cottage. All fabrics, hanging and otherwise, gave off an incense imparted by the many fires of birch and maple. The characteristic scent may have been found in other cottages but, so far as I am concerned, ours was unique, and another signal that I was home.

In the early days at Tanglewood, all the bedrooms except the large one in the

*Buying native crafts from Mr. Benedict. Benedict is at end of dock, surrounded by cottagers.*
– Courtesy Irwin Schultz

attic had only a curtain covering the entryway. Doors were a later luxury. The attic room was reached by a permanent ladder. As members of the family married, putting a strain on the carrying capacity of the house, my grandparents began to spend the night in a capacious tent with a wooden floor. After several years the tent was replaced by a log cabin, the floor of which I helped to lay.

Keeping the larder stocked in those early days must have been a problem. Many kinds of vegetables and canned goods were kept in the "basement," which, because the cottage had been constructed on sloping ground, varied from six feet deep at the front to nil at the rear. I doubt that there was much fresh meat originally, but a steady diet of lake trout — which had disappeared by the time I began fishing in about 1917 — and smallmouth black bass provided the protein. Later, meats were wrapped and buried in the sawdust of the icehouse, which we shared with the Purdys next door. In addition to supplying blocks of ice for refrigeration, I contributed to the warmth by splitting wood and kindling for the almost constantly heated stove and the frequently used fireplaces.

Trips to Huntsville in the launch were made weekly, rain or shine. Thus, some trips were pleasant; others had everyone except perhaps the helmsman covered with oilskins and sheltered by tarps. Such protection was also required on windy days, as the waters of Fairy Lake were sometimes very turbulent.

Shopping excursions followed a rigid schedule in order to allow us to return in good time. The principal concern of my grandfather and me was to be sure we had time to sample the sweets in the soda parlour. Cottagers without motorboats travelled to town and back on the steamer *Algonquin* or relied on the deliveries made by certain merchants in boats of their own. Boyds and Wares would drop around, accept orders at the steamer wharf, and deliver the goods next trip. They announced their arrival by sounding a horn. You would have to drop everything, grab your wallet and meet them, or else your order would return to town.

Our table was also graced by blueberries, raspberries, blackberries, and strawberries. The so-called hay field in back of Tanglewood was a veritable Niagara fruit belt. On each of his biweekly visits, my grandfather would bring up a basket of tomatoes, peaches, cantaloupe, or watermelon, whichever was in season. The contents disappeared quickly.

I don't remember where we got our bread. It may have come with the milk from Bob Wright's farm. A member of his large family used to deposit a quart pail at the back door for breakfast. It knew nothing of pasteurization, but that lack obviously had no adverse effect on my health.

Nor was our drinking water harmful. Springsyde received its name from the number of springs that rose in or near a fern-grown depression in back of the beach. One bubbled up about a hundred feet behind the cottage and flowed down a gully to the lake. There it was impounded in a box from which several cottages drew their water supply. Our supply was trapped at the source and piped to the cottage, giving us, thanks to gravity, running water, although the pressure was not too great.

The customary outhouse was also up the hill, but on the other side of the ridge from the spring. The clay soil made for uncertain footing in wet weather. The privy was not a sumptuous affair, being only a two-holer, but was decorated inside with some of the rotogravure of the day, including copies of more than one masterpiece.

Some items of kitchen waste — rinds, wrappers, boxes, and so forth — were burned in the potbellied stove in the dining room. Every morning at breakfast we had a roaring blaze. Empty cans were tossed into the gully back of the outhouse. I've always thought that future archaeologists would unearth a fantastic tin mine.

The hazards of lighting in those early years were tremendous, yet I am aware of only two fires. One resulted in the total destruction of the Purdys' cottage and the other a similar fate for our boathouse, on the east side of Springsyde Wharf.

Coal-oil lamps were common means of illumination. Most of ours were set in wall brackets or holders and so could not be knocked to the floor. Many had metal reflectors, which greatly magnified the light. The trimming of wicks and polishing of the glass chimneys was a daily task. Less elaborate lamps consisted of a candle within a chimney, while naked candles usually helped one to undress and find the way to bed.

One chore that was particularly tiring, requiring a good deal of muscular effort, was the making of ice cream. Although the result was wonderful, making ice cream by hand was comparable to cutting a lawn with scissors.

Another task, which was sometimes shared, sometimes kept strictly private, was the mail. At the beginning, the cottages at Springsyde rotated mail delivery and collecting. A mounted red mailbox, probably purloined from some civic route, sat on the beach and was the depository for outgoing mail, which was stuffed into a canvas mailbag and handed to the purser on the boat.

Originally, members of the cottage responsible for that day would sort the mail the purser left, then deliver it to the individual cottages. In time, a wall cabinet with labelled pigeonholes was mounted on the inside wall of the wharf. Cottage rotation continued, but the "postmaster" sorted within the shelter, stuffing the mail into the appropriate pigeonholes. In actual practice he had little opportunity to stuff, as the various recipients were often there waiting to claim their letters and packages. The postmaster finally wound up calling out the names of the addressees. He had to contend with a din, the result of comments, shrieks, and laughter as the addressees tore into the epistles. The mail, by the way, would have been posted in Toronto the day before and transported at a cost of two cents a letter and one cent for a postcard!

If time spent at the cottage was fifty per cent working on repairs and expansion and doing chores, the other fifty was taking advantage of the offerings of cottage country. Swimming headed the list, especially for the younger generation. Not many of the older folks could swim, and even if they could, they were hampered by the swimming attire of the day. The women wore what amounted to dresses, complete with skirts. The men donned one-piece suits that covered them from chest to knees. The material in my suit retained moisture so well that drying off in the sun was impossible.

Throughout the day the men's chief activity was fishing, but some afternoons they indulged in a game of horseshoes or quoits. Occasionally the ladies took time off from fighting the vagaries of a wood stove and gathered on someone's verandah to sew, knit, chat, and drink tea.

Idle pleasure was found in rowing or paddling along the shore. The canoe was a popular craft with young couples; a besotted swain sometimes used a double-bladed paddle so that he could face his inamorata. The accepted attire was straw hats and blazers for the men, and billowy dresses and parasols for the ladies, who reclined languidly on cushions, their backs to the bow.

Motor-launch cruises were taken once or twice a season, with Mary Lake or Lake Vernon the destination. If guests were long-staying, they would be treated to an excursion on one of the Lake of Bays steamers.

In the evenings there was little social interchange between neighbors, as walking home over a rock-strewn and root-pitted trail, your way lit only by a flickering hand-held candle lamp, was not pleasant. Instead, the long hours were filled with various card games. In our house, euchre and cribbage prevailed. Reading and sewing were indulged in to some degree, but the comparatively poor lighting soon made the eyes weary.

Bedtime was early, the men tired after hard work or hard rowing to some fishing ground, and the ladies exhausted after their arduous labours in the kitchen. A hot flat iron wrapped in a towel was the most comfortable way to keep feet warm in bed on cold nights.

One event high on the list of recreation was the annual regatta, to which participants and spectators came from afar. The earliest regatta I can remember was 1913, I believe, when I, about five years old, won the sprint through the soft sand of Springsyde beach. I recall only two other incidents from past regattas: the year I took the single-scull prize from Lorne Wright, the perennial winner; and the year a Mansell crew lost the war-canoe race by inches. Our crew consisted of my Uncle Dick in the stern, myself in the bow, and Dick's two sons, Dick and Jack, ten and nine respectively, doing little more than serving as ballast.

The regatta had one sad aspect: it meant that summer was drawing to an end. Soon after the last event, people began closing up their cottages. The season's heat and humidity were history, and cottagers were returning home. Only diehards remained until September.

*William C. Mansell*

# THE MOFFATS

IN THE EARLY 1900s the Moffat brothers and their families began vacationing at Fairy Port, a popular resort on Fairy Lake. During one of these vacations, F.W. Moffat decided to take a skiff and row through the canal into Peninsula Lake. He was so impressed with what he saw that he easily persuaded some of his brothers to explore the lake.

The Springbank shore had recently been subdivided into lots. By 1905 several cottages had already been built.

Three of the five brothers, J.K., T.L., and F.W., purchased adjoining parcels. A fourth parcel, to the west, was purchased in the name of the Moffat Stove Company. It was separated from them by the Ross property, subsequently Rudolph and Edwards.

This last parcel was ultimately bought by the fourth Moffat brother, A.B. (Alfred Bryce). In 1912 A.B. sold his cottage to the remaining brother, C.L. (Charles Lang). (This cottage has since been totally renovated into a fully winterized home and is now owned by the Stevensons.) A.B., who was something of a maverick, moved across the lake and built a cottage, now owned by Don Armstrong, on the Grassmere peninsula.

*Arriving in the* Kanuck.
– Courtesy Bob Moffat

The teenagers spent many enjoyable social hours at A.B.'s, both at Springsyde and at Grassmere. Today, at the old Ashworth cottage, one can still see the marks measuring each child's growth on the two-by-four studs.

Three of the five Moffat brothers married Reid sisters: J.K. married Annie, T.L. married Ella, and C.L. married Ethra. A fourth Reid sister, Ida, married Dr. Jack Fraser and purchased a small, pie-shaped lot subdivided from the original parcel owned by the Moffat Stove Company. This parcel is now owned by Lloyd Brookes.

The Moffats were a closely knit family, sharing and enjoying their summers together. They built a common boathouse on J.K.'s property, in which they kept a shared motor launch, first the *Glasgow* and later the *Kanuck*.

Family gatherings, excursions and fishing were the order of the day. For the women, however, these pleasures were tempered with the many hours spent washing, ironing, putting up preserves, and cooking over a wood-burning stove.

By the late twenties, the families were too large to crowd into the old *Kanuck* and it was replaced by several individually owned smaller boats. When family picnics were planned, they often rented Pow Wow Point Lodge's huge motor

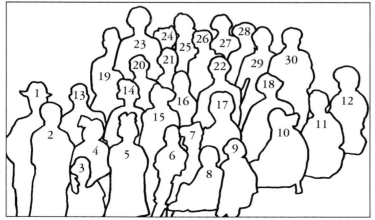

**The Moffat family and friends:**

*1. Thomas Lang Moffat, 2. Charles Moffat, 3 to 6. ?,*
*7. Helen Moffat, 8. Jack Moffat, 9. Don Moffat,*
*10. Dorothy Moffat, 11. ?, 12. Eleanor Bodd, 13. C.L. Moffat, Sr.,*
*14. Eileen Moffat, 15. ?, 16. Bea Moffat, 17. Annie Moffat,*
*18. Jessie Gibson, 19. A.B. Moffat, 20. Ella Moffat, 21. ?,*
*22. Grandma Reid, 23. Emily Wardlaw, 24. Isabelle Moffat,*
*25. Ethra Moffat, 26. ?, 27. Ida Fraser, 28. Miss Duncan,*
*29. ?, 30. Gordon Moffat.*

– Courtesy T.L. Moffat IV

launch, the *Big Chief*. The Moffat grandchildren particularly looked forward to travelling to a picnic at Mary Lake in the *Big Chief*. They loved to hear the loud fire-engine siren announce its arrival.

In 1926 F.W. Moffat decided to give his cottage to his son Jim and to build a new cottage for himself. Consequently, that winter F.W. had his old cottage moved down the hill and across the ice a quarter of a mile to the west to its present location. It has since been fully winterized with a full basement, but the basic structure is virtually unchanged from the original. F.W.'s new cottage was built on the original location and has a commanding view down the lake.

Today only two of the original five Moffat cottages are still owned and enjoyed by members of the Moffat family: Corralyn, the one rebuilt by F.W. in 1926, is owned by F.W.'s daughter, Janet Irwin; and Rothesay, built by J.K. in 1905, is owned by J.K.'s grandson, Bob Moffat.

*RDM*

## SUMMER AT A MISSIONARY COTTAGE

F.W. MOFFAT was a great philanthropist and supporter of the church. Every Sunday morning the family walked to the church services at South Portage, and every Sunday evening a short service was held at F.W.'s cottage. The service consisted of talks, hymns, a slide presentation, and a collection.

Over the years, F.W. visited India and became interested in missionary outreach. He also took a very personal interest in the lives of the missionaries and their families. Around 1915 he purchased land on the Springsyde shore next to Put-in-Bay and erected three cottages. These became known as the missionary cottages, since missionaries home on leave with their families used them during the summer months. The cottages were appropriately named Korea, China, and India. The places have all since been sold to private owners, but the missionary families who once stayed there have not forgotten the pleasures of those long-ago summers. Mary Abrey Hodgins, whose missionary family enjoyed a summer at one of the cottages, has written the following story:

> Over sixty years ago, my parents were invited by Mr. F.W. Moffat to cottage on Peninsula Lake for July. My parents were deeply touched by his generosity and accepted without hesitation. It would be a nice change from our usual summer spot on Muldrew Lake.
>
> Our excitement mounted as time passed. Our only disappointment was that our father was swamped with work and couldn't leave at that time. So my mother, my sister, Marguerite, and I boarded the train to Huntsville on July the first. Once there, we transferred to the *Algonquin*.
>
> I shall never forget that trip. We sat up on deck and drank in the surrounding beauty. The boat stopped at every resort and every dock large enough to accommodate it. At the end of Fairy Lake, we faced an unbroken mass of land.

*The Reid sisters*
*Top: Ida Fraser, Mrs. Reid, Ella Reid,*
*Bottom: Ethra Reid, Annie Reid.*
– Courtesy T.L. Moffat IV family

*Annie Moffat with her son Gordon*
*and a friend. Note the laundry tub on*
*dock, wringer on right, circa 1908.*
– Courtesy Bob Moffat

51

*Rothesay –J.K. Moffat cottage, 1906*
– Courtesy Bob Moffat

We were terrified. Then, the captain skilfully turned the boat into a narrow hidden canal. We brushed against bushes and bulrushes on either side. The captain sounded the horn at every turn to warn oncoming traffic. Finally, Penlake opened before us.

Our cottage was rustic, surrounded by fir, birch, and oak. A path in front of us opened to the lake. Heaven!

Our host, Mr. Moffat, visited us the next day. He was small and bronzed by the sun, lean and wiry with a shock of pure white curly hair. He wore only white shorts and running shoes. He attributed his physical fitness to a rigid diet. Five years previously, doctors had told him he had only one year to live, so he switched to a wonder diet he had heard about. As a result, he became right as rain!

Mother, too, had given up on doctors. She was on a strict diet to alleviate her crippling arthritis. They compared notes and found that their diets were similar, except that Mother's was far less restrictive. Mr. Moffat was delighted. He had a buddy! Each day, he bore gifts from his organic garden: fresh vegetables and jars of soup made from carrot tops, dandelions and potato plants. He had his own grist mill and clay oven from which he produced loaves of bread which were a real test for the jaws. Mother was pleased, but did not inflict her diet on the family; we were perfectly healthy.

Many incorrectly think that all missionaries are ministers. All are steeped in theology and are highly motivated, but most have practical skills for the missionary community. Our

*The original Corralyn, the F.W. Moffat cottage prior to its 1926 move down the lake.*
– Courtesy Nancy Moffat Scarth

neighbours in the other missionary cottages included a doctor and a professor. My father was an architect who planned and oversaw the building of homes, an infirmary, schoolhouse, chapel, etc. He could also preach a fine sermon. He and Mother had served in west China, and both spoke Mandarin fluently.

Every Sunday Mr. Moffat ferried the missionaries to a church service which was held in the open pavilion at the golf course. I was captivated by the surroundings. Nature and all its glories lent so much to the services. I was just eleven or twelve but felt very close to heaven. Then, wonder of wonders, a young man sang a solo in a magnificent tenor voice. His name was Si Hodgins. In about ten years, he became my father-in-law!

In the evenings, I often took the old barge of a rowboat and rowed straight out and around the island a good distance away. On the way back, I rested on the oars and watched the sun in all its brilliance sink behind the far-off twin hills.

Bless you, Mr. Moffat, for making this lovely summer possible!

# THE DILWORTHS'
## EARLY YEARS AT COME HITHER

My FATHER CAME TO PENINSULA LAKE in 1904 with my mother, and they stayed on Isle Dunelg with her cousin, George Richardson. He owned the island with his friend, Robert James Berkinshaw, who brought in his partner, Eugene Henderson. Later the island was divided into three properties, with the Ogle family taking over Mr. Berkinshaw's interest.

In 1908 we tented in the peafield — which later became the golf course — and Father found a property he liked. That winter, he went to Huntsville and persuaded Mr. Casselman to sell him three lots on the south shore east of Pym's Point. The lawyer who witnessed the sale was Colonel Donald McKenzie Grant, who promptly bought two lots to the west of ours.

Our cottage was built in 1909 by E.S. Brooks, owner of the sawmill in Grassmere. It was a two-storey affair with pine siding. There were four bedrooms upstairs, a large living room downstairs with a stone fireplace, a kitchen with a wood-burning stove, and a small pantry. We ate most of our meals on a large verandah, L-shaped at the west end, which spanned the front. The cottage cost Father $525, plus $30 for a dock and $8 for a two-holer. A boathouse was added in 1910.

We had coal-oil lamps and candles in Chinese lanterns. A hand pump with a storage tank on the hill behind the house provided the kitchen with running water. Each of us did fifty strokes a day and double on wash days, and brought

*Tent interior at the peafield.*
*Note the kerosene container*
*for fueling the stove.*
– Courtesy Sylvia Hurst-Brown

wood for the stove, which had a large container on one end for water. So we had both hot and cold in the kitchen, and on Saturday night, in a big washtub in the kitchen, we'd have our weekly scrub.

We shopped in Huntsville for some of our provisions. Milk, cream, ice, and fresh vegetables and fruit were brought by boat from Mr. Morgan's farm in the canal several times a week. It was a delightful sight, with the stern deck neatly displaying his colourful garden produce. Under the cover of the boat roof were blocks of ice in sawdust and large cans of milk, cream, and butter, which he measured out into whatever containers we supplied.

In 1914 a bushfire west of Pym's Point ravaged about an acre of hillside. In a panic, Mrs. Grant rolled two large drums of gasoline into the lake (her husband kept them for the launch in which he commuted to work in Huntsville). Fortunately the fire was contained and no buildings were destroyed.

We spent our days swimming and boating, and many hours fishing. I enjoyed the early morning paddle to the canal to shoot bullfrogs and retrieve them before they sank. Frog legs in place of fish was a treat for me, though my sister, Rosalind, was revolted!

From 1910 on we used Deerhurst Inn as a postal address through the kindness of the owner, Mr. Waterhouse, until a post office was established at North Portage.

Logging on the lake was constant, and numerous booms were towed down the lake to Huntsville by the sturdy tugboat *Phoenix*. My younger brother, Paul, used to hitch his canoe to the boom, and while chewing tobacco with the crew of loggers, increased his vocabulary considerably.

Mr. Fisher lived across the lake at Pow Wow Point. While not known for his own morals, he was very strict with his daughter. Once when leaving her at the dock after an outing, my older brother, Ralph, was fired upon as he retreated by canoe across the lake!

In 1928 we were finally able to drive right to the cottage. In 1933 Father had the cottage razed and a new one built. It had a partial basement for a hot-air furnace and electricity throughout. There was no more cleaning and filling of lamps, trimming wicks, and pumping water.

While the house was being built, we lived in the front cabin, number one, and cooked in the boathouse, which had been enlarged to include two slips, a work area, and two change rooms. The new house had four bedrooms upstairs, each with a basin with hot and cold water, and one common toilet. Downstairs was a large L-shaped living-dining room with a stone fireplace. A verandah was off the west end. Behind the fireplace was a big kitchen and a small porch. A bedroom with screened porch and full bathroom were off the hall.

With the advent of the golf course and an increasing number of cottagers, we not only had tournaments at Penlake, but engaged yearly in matches with the guests at Bigwin Inn. As we could only muster six to eight players and Bigwin

*The first Come Hither,*
*Dilworth cottage.*
– Courtesy Sylvia Hurst-Brown

had a choice of many, some of championship stature, it was very one-sided, but we had a great time and lots of laughs.

At a time when women smoking was accepted in England, and some of the male players smoked cigarettes, our players were slightly shocked when, on one occasion, Jean McCready took her husband's pipe and put it in her mouth. She walked solemnly up to the tee, placed the pipe on the sandbox, drove, then retrieved the pipe and strolled down the fairway (albeit only eight feet, for she wasn't much of a player), to the delight of the watching crowd.

In later years we amused ourselves with square dancing. It was good exercise and some of us became very proficient. Many a Saturday night we "tore apart" Walker's Lake or South Portage halls with our exuberance.

*Sylvia (Dilworth) Hurst-Brown*

## MEMORIES OF EULA (FOSTER) CAMPBELL
*from a 1976 interview with Douglas G. Darling*

*D.D.: Fifty-five years ago, you came from Toronto to a place called Pow Wow. Tell me, how did you decide to come here?*

E.C.: My husband and I used to go fishing in the summer. After my daughter was born, we felt we couldn't take a young baby to fishing camps. My husband saw an ad in the paper about a wonderful cottage with hot running water and electricity. It was owned by Mr. A.B. Fisher, who called the cottage Bluebird. On their curtains they had stencilled bluebirds on a white scrim. It was a very attractive cottage. Eventually, it became Pow Wow Lodge. We had it for three years before we left there and moved to Inkerman, a cottage on the other side of the lake.

*D.D.: From Pow Wow you went to Inkerman. Where did you go from there?*

E.C.: We were one year at Inkerman, and then we came over and had a cottage at Winoka. It was Mrs. Winchester's, and we were in that cottage for about five years. Then we went to one that Miss Hill, a schoolteacher, had built, up near the golf links. Very often we'd go out to that tee just where the cottage was and watch people as they were coming around to play. When we rented it, there was nothing in it, only a double brass bed. So we had to buy a stove and refrigerator, and we had to furnish it. Very often, I'd bring something up from my home, something that I was discarding, but our car would be laden with things we were bringing to finish this cottage. It would make my husband so annoyed that we had to bring so much.

*D.D.: How did you get there?*

E.C.: We came by train to Pow Wow. The roads weren't fit. We couldn't take the motor car and the sand was so deep. We'd leave Toronto by train by about eleven in the morning and have our lunch on the train — go into the dining room and

*Paul Dilworth,*
*with a long-stroke pump.*
– Courtesy Sylvia Hurst-Brown

56

enjoy it very much. We'd arrive up in Huntsville about three, and usually take the *Algonquin* to Penlake. In those years, it'd stop right at Pow Wow.

We were up here about six years before we motored up. Each year we'd have to come by train, and sometimes we'd have the Blackburn boat people bring us out in a launch to our cottage instead of going all around the lake on the big boat.

**D.D.: *We were telling stories earlier today that you would sneak things out and put them on the front lawn to get them into the car, just leaving a little pile of things that had to go.***

E.C.: When my daughter was about five, she had some little chicks she wanted to bring. We put them in a box and we had them on the running board of the car. We had to put a little window in the orange crate so that the mother hen could see her chicks. On the way up, the hen laid an egg. We had a very lovely dog named Silk. We'd have to stop at every little river and give him a drink. You could put a suitcase along the running board of the car. Often some of your supplies could go on that, too. But, oh, when we were coming to Muskoka, we'd have to get oil three or four times. My husband would carry a pair of overalls so that when he had to get out to fix a tire, he'd have those overalls to put on.

We'd always go to Eaton's in Toronto and buy a lot of our groceries because it was hard to get things at Penlake, although small boats did come in with supplies of fresh vegetables.

**D.D.: *Did you rely on these people who came around with vegetables for most of your shopping?***

E.C.: When they'd come, we'd buy their vegetables. Then native Indians came around with baskets for sale made of sweet-smelling grass. I have some of the doilies that they sold. But we were rather afraid of them because we didn't see many of them.

There was a church not far away, the Hillside United Church. We'd occasionally go there. The ministers coming to the lake were very good, so often one of them would preach in the golf course pavilion. If there was a good singer on the lake, why, he'd maybe sing a solo and Mrs. Henderson would play the piano. They had a big square piano in the pavilion at that time.

**D.D.: *Where would the meat come from?***

E.C.: Huntsville, but sometimes various farmers would kill a lamb or a calf, and we'd get roasts and some veal from them. There is nothing like Muskoka lamb.

**D.D.: *When you got to the cottage, how often would you go to Huntsville?***

E.C.: In the years when we came by train, if we got into Huntsville twice in the season, that would be all. We'd have to go in the big boat. But one time when we had been on the lake about three years, an American who had driven up from his home in the States took Anna Mirrette and me into Huntsville. We never, never

*Girls rafting in 1910 - Ida Dilworth.*
– Courtesy Sylvia Hurst-Brown

thought of going to the movies in Huntsville. We didn't know whether they had movies or not.

D.D.: *You used to bring up hired help at that time, too.*

E.C.: Oh, yes, often. Sometimes two maids — I know that when my baby was small, we had two. One to look after her and the other to do the cooking. We'd have girls from the Old Country as summer help. The night after we arrived, the farm boys would always come over to meet the girls. Some of these girls wouldn't know not to step on the edge or back of a canoe as they were getting in. The thing would tip into the water, and they'd have to come to the house and get all dry clothes on before they could go out with the young men for the evening.

D.D.: *How much did you have to pay a maid in those days?*

E.C.: Maybe $15 for the housemaid, and perhaps $16 or $20 for the cook — for a month. That was the price. When we came on the lake, George Hill, who had one of the best farms, would bring eggs. I think they were only 25 cents a dozen for large eggs. You could get a cabbage for five cents. You could feed a whole family of five for 25 cents.

D.D.: *Well, tell me, with the two maids, what did* you *do?*

E.C.: Just played golf and enjoyed myself. [*Laughter.*] That's the reason I had a few good years, but when the Depression came things weren't so rosy, because we had a lot of stocks and bonds and they were eaten up.

D.D.: *Did many people have boats, or did you rely on the steamer?*

E.C.: When we took the first cottage, we had quite a big launch. My husband didn't know very much about driving it and we had a bank manager staying with us, but we went out in it. We didn't know there were big rocks up near the Portage, and we got stuck on those rocks. It's well we weren't lost, but someone came to our rescue, and we managed to get off these big rocks without doing any damage to the boat. At the second cottage, we had a "dispro" boat [disappearing- propeller boat].

D.D.: *What did you do for transportation? I can't visualize you driving a DP.*

E.C.: No, I didn't, but I had a rowboat, and it was all I could do to get that rowboat into the boathouse. [*Laughter.*]

We enjoyed life on the lake very much. We were both fond of golf, my husband and I, and so in time, he and three other men bought the golf course, in 1929. They paid $30,000 for it. We played golf nearly every day.

D.D.: *How did the golf course get started? That was what year?*

E.C.: Oh, it had started before we were here. We came here in 1920 and Mr. Henderson owned it. It was a nine-hole course. When my husband and these three

Americans bought it, they thought that they must have an eighteen-hole course right away. They had to buy the road into the golf links and all the lots along the shore — four lots. But after the balmy days of the twenties, the Depression came, and they never finished the golf course.

**D.D.: *How much did your annual membership cost you?***

E.C.: I think $15. I think it was just a dollar a day to play, but the greens were kept in good condition and it was all in very fine shape.

I don't like to brag, but at golf, I think I was champion twice and I think my daughter was champion twice of the Penlake golf club. But it's just too bad that the scroll was burned about two years ago, although I have, and my daughter has, the cups that we've won.

**D.D.: *Did you have a regatta then?***

E.C.: They always had one around Civic Holiday. All the children would take part, and sometimes I'd go in the nail-driving contest. I didn't go in the swimming, because as a child I hadn't learned to swim well. One summer at the regatta, there were some people visiting Penlake from New York, and one lady asked my husband if he'd go into this tilting race with her. She wanted very much to be in it. But my husband was a very gentle, kind man and he said, "Oh no, I couldn't go into a tilting race and punch at a woman."

But he would take her fishing, because he was an ardent fisherman. If there were fish to be caught, Archie Campbell would catch them. At night, he'd go out to get little crawfish as bait. I think that was the secret of his success, because many times he'd get all that you're allowed to get in about an hour. The strange part of it was he didn't care to eat the fish. Yet he'd sit for hours, fishing. Penlake is very deep at points. Over at Pym's Point, he could put a copper line down and you couldn't touch bottom. I think there were so many smallmouth bass because the water was so cold down there. Deerhurst gave prizes or cups for the largest fish, and two or three times Archie won them.

**D.D.: *What are some of the early resorts?***

E.C.: In those days, a great many people went to Bigwin Inn for their holidays, up in Lake of Bays. It was a very popular place and expensive. It was owned by Mr. Shaw who had a tannery in Huntsville. He had, amongst his employees, his own band. This band would often play at Bigwin Inn.

*A.W. Campbell catching crawfish.*
– Courtesy Anna Mirrette Darling

About a year after we left Pow Wow, Mr. Fisher turned it into an inn. Cedar Grove was here, as well as Grandview and Deerhurst. When we were at Pow Wow we got our mail at Deerhurst. We went over there every Sunday for dinner. Mr. Waterhouse, an Englishman, was the host. He'd sing his English songs and was very entertaining.

*D.D.: You'd like to talk about berries.*

E.C.: My husband was very fond of picking berries, but I wasn't. Really, if I got a cup of berries in half a day, I was lucky. I'd eat too many! He was a wonderful picker. There were big, high hills across from Pow Wow. He'd go over there and find plenty of raspberries in season and pick enough that we'd be able to make jam. The side of the hill was just covered in fruits of all kinds. He liked picking berries, but I never did.

When I'd come to the lake, often my sister and her husband from Pittsburgh would come to Tally Ho. That was very pleasant, to have them so near, and they'd always have a boat. In fact they brought their own engine with them and attached it to an outboard. They had to bring it across the border.

After my brother, George Foster, was married, he came to Deerhurst and brought his wife, Eleanor. They liked it so much that when a lot was for sale, he bought it. A man by the name of Petersen built the cottage for my brother. It was a very well-built cottage. Mr. Petersen also made very attractive, hand-painted stools, something like a milking stool, and all my guests who would come to visit me, they'd always go and buy one. The Fosters encouraged many of their friends to purchase property here — Johnny Hay, who later married Trudy Spurr, the Todds, Dr. and Mrs. Weaber.

*D.D.: What was the social life like?*

E.C.: We'd have bridge parties and the ladies would have teas. Then on one night in the summer, the men would put on a dinner over at the clubhouse. It was really a wonderful dinner. That was for people who belonged to the clubhouse. In the early days, we didn't have a lake association and many people who used the golf links road, they were supposed, if they had a cottage along the road, to pay us some small amount each year for the upkeep of that road.

*D.D.: Are you sorry you never built a cottage?*

E.C.: Oh, yes, I regret it terribly, but as things turned out, I think it was just as well, because when we felt the pinch we might have had to give it up. That would have been very difficult.

# PENLAKE RESORTS

## PORTAGE LODGE

Not too much is known about the old
Portage Lodge. Built in the 1880s with wood
brought in by barge, the lodge was probably
used by loggers working in the area.

In the 1890s and early 1900s it was a popular stopping point on the trip between North
and South Portage. Before the advent of the
Little Train, this trip was made by horse-drawn
wagon.

The *Portage Flyer* brought with it the danger
of small bushfires caused by sparks thrown off
by the engines. At one point the tracks ran
close to the lodge. It was not uncommon to see
the guests rushing out of the lodge to extin-
guish a small blaze.

In 1941 the Walker family bought the lodge
from the Allisons. They named it Walker's
Lodge and ran it as a family resort. At that time, Mrs. Walker did all the cooking.
The cost of staying there ran as high as $25 a week, but of course this included all
meals!

*Portage Lodge in 1923*
– Courtesy Don Marshall

In 1960 the Walkers sold the lodge to the Knotts, who cut down all the trees
and dismantled the porch before defaulting on the mortgage. The Walkers repossessed it, then sold it to people from Windsor, who also defaulted. The lodge was
repossessed a second time. When the Walkers sold the property for the third time,
to John Turner, they refused to take back a mortgage.

John Turner turned the lodge into a disco for teenagers. After he was charged
with breaking the anti-noise bylaw, he closed the disco and later sold the place to
Bill Sloan and his wife. They operated an exclusive women's health spa there for
two years before putting the place on the market again. In August 1992 it was
sold to the Dearings, who plan to turn it into a restaurant.

*as told by Bob Walker to RDM*

# DEERHURST INN

CHARLES WATERHOUSE, a young Englishman who immigrated to Canada in 1896, established Deerhurst Inn as a fishing lodge open for two months of the year.

On a summer day in 1904 Harry Wadsworth and his American-born wife, Laura, great-grandparents of Jamee Todd, were aboard the *Algonquin*, bound for a resort destination, when she docked temporarily at Deerhurst Inn. While there, Harry met and took an immediate liking to fellow Englishman Charles Waterhouse. Harry ordered their luggage removed from the boat, and the Wadsworths spent their vacation at Deerhurst.

Thus began an extended family presence on Penlake that lasted until 1971. The Wadsworth, Littleford, Heinze, and Stegeman cousins sometimes comprised as many as fifty guests at Deerhurst Inn. With the permission of Deerhurst, Harry Wadsworth and brother-in-law John Littleford built their own cottages on the Deerhurst lakefront. When they were not at the cottages, Deerhurst Inn rented them to guests.

When Charlie Waterhouse retired in 1921, his son, Maurice, managed the inn, by then a full-fledged summer resort. Recalling the regatta motorboat races, Maurice said that when people first got five- and ten-horsepower motors, he thought they would "tear up the lake." He remembered how people used to make

### "DEERHURST"
### SCHEDULE OF RATES

**South and West Exposures**

| | |
|---|---|
| Single Rooms | $35.00 per week |
| Double Rooms (two people) | $32.00 per week per person |

**North Exposure**

| | |
|---|---|
| Single Rooms | $31.00 per week |
| Double Rooms (two people) | $28.00 per week per person |

**Cottages**

Cottages rent for from $25.00 to $50.00 per week, plus $28.00 per week per person for meals, cottage service, fire wood, etc.
One room bungalows $10.00 and two room bungalows $15.00 per week, plus $28.00 per week per person.
Children under thirteen years of age pay full rate less $7.00 per week.

**Boats and Canoes**

| | |
|---|---|
| $7.00 per week | $1.50 per day |

*Rates of yesteryear!*

– Courtesy the Spurr family

*Deerhurst Inn*
– Courtesy Anna Mirrette Darling

*Tennis at Deerhurst in the early 1900s.*
– Courtesy Lake of Bays, Highlands of Ontario, issued by the Grand Trunk Railway, Montreal, 1909

their own fun: holding torchlight parades using torches made from cattails cut in the canal and soaked in kerosene; towing logs by canoe; building twenty-foot bonfires that would burn for three or four days; and taking part in singsongs. In 1971 Maurice turned over the management of Deerhurst to his son, Bill, and retired to a cottage near Tally Ho.

In the same year, Bill Waterhouse and a group of associates completely renovated the hotel to facilitate year-round operation.

With the completion of the 1990 Deerhurst expansion, the inn, with 370 guest rooms, has become the largest resort in Ontario, providing a wide range of recreational, entertainment, and conference facilities.

Deerhurst Inn occupies an extensive shoreline and two former farms owned by the Farnsworth and Turnbull families. According to the Crown-land-grants map of Chaffey Township, the property on the north shore of Peninsula Lake near the canal originally belonged to J. Hood. Sometime later it became a farm owned by Mr. Turnbull. Jack Turnbull, a son, now lives at Ballantine Heights near Novar. A portion of the Turnbull property and the entire neighbouring farm, owned by the Farnsworths, were sold to Deerhurst Inn in the 1950s. The Turnbulls divided the shore property into cottage lots.

*Joan Miles*

# TALLY HO INN

*In the early days, the Indians had a camping ground right where Tally Ho Inn is now. When Hugh Hill was about fifteen, he used to plow that ground on his dad's farm and would plow out skinning stones, tomahawks and arrowheads. At that age he did not pay much attention to them, but in later years he saved several. He gave them away to their visitors from the United States.*

*Hugh Hill,*
*from "My Grandfather's Early Days in Muskoka"*

*Tally Ho Inn in 1936*
— Courtesy Anna Mirrette Darling

AT ONE TIME there was a sawmill on the property, owned by E.S. Brooks. The inn — originally called Wequash, which meant "white duck" — was operated by Mr. and Mrs. Jack Robinson, and then by Mr. and Mrs. Gordon Hill, who founded Limberlost. Mrs. Hill changed the name to Tally Ho and had the inn managed, in turn, by Dorothy Kitchen, Major Ernie Gunn — a particularly genial host — Agnes Kearns, and Clara Rose.

In 1939 Betty and Isabel Emberson bought and took over the operation of Tally Ho. They were two of the five Emberson sisters who for many years successfully operated the Five Sisters Tea Room on Roncesvalles Avenue in Toronto.

Betty and Isabel were assisted by their sister Mrs. Sharp, whose son Colin built and operated the Horseshoe Snack Bar across the road and west of Tally Ho. The Horseshoe, a popular spot for many years, was patronized by locals, cottagers, and Tally Ho guests alike as *the* place to purchase a late-night snack. It has changed hands several times over the years, and its current incarnation is the Hillside Bistro and Art Gallery.

When the Embersons ran Tally Ho, they encouraged their guests to paint the local scenery. Many of these paintings were donated to the hotel and hung on the dining-room walls. Among the artists was Marjorie Pigott, who later became quite famous.

Betty Emberson married Ted West. Today Andrew West owns the hotel.

*AMD*

# POW WOW POINT LODGE

THE LAND ON WHICH POW WOW POINT LODGE STANDS was well known to the people of the First Nations long before there was a cottage or resort there. The site was used for powwow — which means meetings, or gatherings.

Alex Fisher bought the property in 1920. A man of great imagination, he invented the Fisher tube skates and a machine that formed and wrapped a five-cent chocolate bar called Bluebird, which is the name Fisher chose for his cottage at Pow Wow Point. He also obtained the rights to manufacture the Waterman engine in Canada. He called it the Kingfisher. This engine was used in most Canadian DPs, or dispros. Shortly after building a cottage on his new property, he saw it as an ideal spot for a Muskoka resort.

When Alex set his creative mind to that, he achieved a charming blend of rustic log cabins, each of which was appointed with the latest in conveniences: hot and cold running water and flush toilets. A Delco plant generated electricity to provide all these amenities when his first guests arrived in 1930.

*Pow Wow Point*
– Courtesy Anna Mirrette Darling

Hospitality was the key to Fisher's early success as an innkeeper. This he achieved with the help of Betty and Isabel Emberson, who were experienced in the art of making guests feel welcome.

Alex also purchased a forty-two-foot launch, the *Big Chief*, which quickly became the pride of the north Muskoka lakes. It ferried new arrivals from the train in Huntsville to their final destination at Pow Wow.

When Alex died in 1938, a conflict arose over the settlement of his estate, and the Supreme Court of Ontario was called upon to resolve it. The resort was then purchased by Douglas Fairly, who also owned the Royal Muskoka Lodge. The Emberson sisters, now entrenched in the resort trade, purchased Tally Ho Inn from Gordon Hill. Douglas added improvements to Pow Wow and, as he was involved in theatre in the Niagara area, was able to attract a number of theatre people and residents of the Niagara Peninsula.

During the Second World War, John B. Lobe assumed ownership of the lodge. As this was the era of the seaplane, he installed large floating docks to accommodate the arrival of at least a dozen aircraft. Comedians Abbott and Costello, who were entertaining at the Canadian National Exhibition, came to Pow Wow by seaplane for a day of rest. Apparently, during the shore approach, which was a little precipitous, a pontoon was punctured. No repairs were possible during the comedians' brief visit. Upon their return to Toronto, they had to make a very hasty exit from the plane after it landed at Toronto Island Airport, because it promptly sank. Not to waste a good story, Abbott and Costello turned the event into a riotous skit, which few people realized was based on experience.

In 1948 a Mr. Brown and Sam Vale purchased Pow Wow Point Lodge. They bought a Shepherd inboard launch at the end of the CNE ski show that year so that guests could be treated to flamboyant displays of waterskiing. Guests and many cottagers especially remember when Sam and company skied around the peninsula dressed as a bride and groom!

In 1954 the Chaloner family purchased Pow Wow. In 1962 Misses Ida and Dorothy Chaloner first opened for the winter season, in the wake of Hidden Valley's development as a ski area.

Jack and Jacquie Howell noted: "We had the pleasure of being winter guests on several occasions...and during our last visit, learned that the resort was for sale." They purchased the lodge soon afterward, on August 5, 1969.

A second generation of "Howell hospitality" continues to provide all the comforts of a modern resort while preserving past traditions. Now open year-round, Pow Wow Point Lodge remains a meeting place worthy of the name — beyond Alex Fisher's wildest dreams.

*Meg Giller, and Jack and Jacquie Howell*

*The* **Big Chief** *was the*
*Pow Wow Point launch.*
– Courtesy the Rev. J.K. Moffat family

## CEDAR GROVE LODGE

THE ORIGINAL CEDAR GROVE LODGE PROPERTY was purchased by Hugh Buster Fleming from his father, Hugh Fleming, Sr., in 1930. The son's dream started small, with one hand-built log cabin. Trees had to be floated to the sawmill at the locks to be sawed into lumber. Hugh spent the first few summers developing the property. Winters were spent in Detroit automobile factories working to raise cash. In 1932 the resort opened full-time. Even though the Depression was at its worst, people from the city still sought refuge at Peninsula Lake. To supplement their income during the lean winter months, the Flemings cut ice from the lake and placed it in the ice huts of neighbouring cottages.

Buster's marriage to Evelyn Fowler in 1940 really started the family-resort tradition. Vacations at that time were never less than two to four weeks in duration. As Muskoka was the honeymoon destination of choice during the 1940s and 1950s, May and June became just as busy as July and August are now.

In 1945 Cedar Grove started one of the first truck-operated ski hills in Ontario. The lift was in operation until 1963, charging a mere dollar a day. Along with Limberlost and Huntsville Ski Club, Cedar Grove was the origin of present-day winter business in Muskoka.

The business is now owned by Gary and Barbara Fleming, who carry on the long-standing tradition of Muskoka hospitality.

*Gary and Barbara Fleming*

*Lovebird cabin at Cedar Grove*
– From the Cedar Grove brochure

# FRIENDLY ACRES

THE FRIENDLY ACRES FARM was part of the original land grant to Rev. Norton Hill. He deeded it to his son, Joseph, who in turn passed it on to his son, Hugh.

In the 1920s and 1930s Hugh Hill had several riding horses for hire on his farm. Many cottagers enjoyed the friendly atmosphere of the stables and pleasant rides with Hugh, George Hinton, or Hugh's daughter, Lorraine ("Toots"). There were many treks, including all-day outings to Limberlost and the sawdust trail to Walker Lake sawmill.

Elspeth Ashworth Armstrong recalls this sawmill as "an absolutely fascinating place. Many cottagers would ride to the mill, going up the Limberlost road, past the Fleming farm, to a sawdust trail. The road wound through damp, almost swampy woods, over a creek and finally to the mill. The sawdust made a great surface to walk and ride on when it was packed down and damp. All sorts of wonderful fungi grew along the road.

"The mill was not used in summer. We could climb all over it. It was built right against a high, sheer cliff. Farther along, the cliff was lower. A ladder enabled us to climb to the top. There, a few yards off, lay Walker's Lake. A channel supplied water to a huge iron pipe which ran down the cliff, delivering the water to run the machinery. When the mill was not in use, the water was blocked off at the top. Sometime during or after the Second World War, the mill machinery was sold. The mill fell into ruin and disappeared."

In the early 1940s the family farm became the resort Friendly Acres. Hugh Hill subdivided the lakeshore lots, retaining beach facilities for his guests. The stately farmhouse became the lodge. He built several cabins and winterized the barn, adding a recreation room. Friendly Acres was renowned for its genial hospitality and delicious home-cooked meals. The likable Andrew "Scotty" Murray was the hired hand. The original smaller house by the highway was the home of Mr. and Mrs. Joe Hill, and even after her husband's death Mrs. Hill continued to live there for many years.

When Hugh and his wife, Florence, decided to retire, Toots and her husband, Aage Petersen, continued to operate Friendly Acres.

The Hillside United Church Ladies' Pancake Frolic was an annual event at Friendly Acres. It was held once in July and again in August. Delicious pancakes were cooked in a field kitchen by the ladies of the auxiliary. Guests participated in pickup games of baseball and horseshoes. Sometimes there was an auction sale — an event so popular that other events on the lake were scheduled so as not to conflict with it.

Friendly Acres has always been involved with the community. In later years, under the management of Jan and Tom Roberts, Friendly Acres provided space and facilities for the annual corn roast of the Peninsula Lake Association after the golf course clubhouse burned down.

The resort is now closed. Only the housekeeping cabins are rented, and these on a more permanent basis.

*Elspeth Ashworth Armstrong, ISA and AMD*

# COLONIAL BAY RESORT

THIS ESTABLISHMENT, consisting of several cabins and a motor court, is owned and operated by Lyle Henry. Previously it was located south of Huntsville, but that site was expropriated when Highway 11 was widened several years ago. Subsequently the resort opened at its present location.

*AMD*

# HIDDEN VALLEY RESORT HOTEL

HIGH ON A HILL overlooking the lake is the Hidden Valley Resort Hotel. Built in the 1960s, it is the most recent large resort in the area. Hidden Valley began as a part of the Holiday Inn group, but has had various operators over the years. At present, it is owned by the Rose Corporation and franchised to Best Western. There are a hundred guest rooms, an indoor-outdoor swimming pool, whirlpool, sauna, and a restaurant.

The resort includes a number of townhouses, which sit halfway down the hillside from the hotel. A few are privately owned and all have a beautiful view of the lake. The hotel is adjacent to the Hidden Valley Ski Club property, which is owned by its members. Both the ski club and the hotel are on points of land between Grace's Bay and Morgan's Bay, named after the original holders of the Crown grants. Today, the area is referred to as Hidden Valley Bay.

*AMD*

# L I F E   O N   T H E   L A K E

## D A I L Y   L I V I N G

To the Penlake pioneers, daily living meant a lot of hard work just to obtain life's necessities. They had to be self-reliant for food and shelter. They built their own cabins, often with the help of family and friends. They also planted their own gardens. A cash crop was required for trade or barter. Some worked as loggers or millers to make ends meet.

If one could afford a cow and some chickens, so much the better. Milk and cream from the cow was used for drink and cooking. The settlers churned butter and made cheese. A pig was a good investment, as it didn't require much to feed and in the end provided meat. A root cellar near the cabin stored potatoes, carrots, turnips, and apples for winter use. The only refrigeration was an icebox — when blocks of ice became available. Before that, the cottager relied on a nearby cave or cool stream.

Drinking water was provided by springs and was carried in buckets or pumped to a reservoir by hand. Firewood was felled and cut on the property for heat and cooking. Homemade candles and coal-oil lamps lit the cabins. Settlers baked their own bread and pies. They picked berries and gathered wild plants for jams, jellies, and preserves. Dandelions were a source of fresh greens.

Hugh Hill remembers native Canadians coming to his father's home, walking in the door without knocking, and talking in a language he couldn't understand. They would exchange venison, fish, and other foods for tea and sugar, and such staples as the Reverend might have.

When the cottagers began to arrive in the early years of this century, transportation improved. They were able to bring more provisions and comforts with them by rail and boat. But cooking, whether on a wood, propane, or kerosene stove, was still a chore.

Cottagers employed several methods of doing the laundry, from washing in the lake to agitating the water in a tub with a plunger or a rotator. They shaved and dissolved soap. Clothes were wrung out by hand or passed through a wringer. It's no wonder that on "wash day" the family fare was simple!

Frequently the following day was "ironing day." A flat iron was heated on the stove, passed over the clothing, and reheated for the next item.

Coal-oil lamps required daily care: trimming the wicks, cleaning the glass

*Fetching water in 1910.*
*Note spring and root cellar*
*in background.*
– Courtesy the Moffat family

chimneys, and replenishing the oil. Coleman lamps had to be refilled with naptha, and broken mantles had to be replaced. Because of the high risk of fire, lighting the lamps was a job entrusted only to adults. The task was always performed outside. After air was pumped into the naptha, a valve was opened, and then a lighted match applied to the hissing rush of fuel and air passing over the mantle. A great gush of flame arose, which could then be controlled by turning the valve until the little stocking-like mantle glowed with a much brighter light than that provided by coal oil or candle.

A good wood supply was always essential to the early cottagers. Usually it was ordered from a local farmer and came in different sizes and lengths: split logs for the fireplace, shorter pieces for the stove, kindling for both. Many a man and boy spent their time chopping wood for the woodpile and filling the wood boxes by the stove and fireplace. The wood stove seemed to burn constantly.

*Wash day. Note the milk jugs.*
– Courtesy the T.L. Moffat family

Each shore had a local iceman who would store ice, which was cut from the lake in winter, in sawdust in the cottagers' icehouses. Every few days the cottager would move a fifty-pound block of ice from the icehouse, wash it free of sawdust, and use heavy tongs to carry it to the icebox on the back porch or the coolest place handy to the kitchen. If there was no icebox, such perishables as milk, butter, eggs, and vegetables were stored in caves near cottages or in watertight boxes placed in cool springs. Meat and fish were often wrapped well and stored in the icehouse, which was kept closed and cool. As the ice became used up toward the end of the summer and the pile of sawdust increased, the kids had fun cavorting in it — especially on a hot day. The sawdust was so damp and cool!

Garbage was another chore for the early cottager. Usually a deep pit was dug, and a wooden cover made to keep animals away. Mostly tin cans and bottles were thrown into the pit, while food scraps and paper were burned, either in the fireplace, stove, or an outside incinerator. Evening was the most popular time for these garbage fires, and smoke from them could be seen drifting all over the lake.

*The Spurr cottage shuttered for the winter.*
– Courtesy Whitney Holloway

Supply boats from the farmers and Huntsville merchants took orders and brought milk, butter, eggs, and vegetables to the cottagers. There was a store and post office at North Portage in the early 1920s, and Mrs. Knud Petersen opened a grocery store and post office at Hillside in the 1930s.

Cottagers took the *Algonquin* or *Ramona* steamboat, or sometimes a launch, to shop in Huntsville. By the late 1920s the roads were good enough to drive to town.

Keeping mice, raccoons, skunks, and ground-hogs away from food has always been a challenge to the cottager. However, in the early days, cottages were much more vulnerable to invasion by mice. Of course mousetraps were widely employed, but the biggest problem was mouse-proofing the cottage for the winter, when it sat vacant. And so closing cottages at the end of the season entailed a great deal of work. Food was taken away. Materials such as linens, blankets, pillows, and curtains were stored in mouse-proof boxes, sometimes in tin-lined cupboards. Mattresses were piled on tabletops in the centre of the living room. Table legs were designed to make them impossible for mice to climb. Even dishes, lamp shades, and rugs needed protective storage. When all was finished, the windows were shuttered and the doors securely closed. Cottagers could only hope that when they returned in the spring, the tiny mauraders had written their place off as a bad bet!

*Cross-cut saw at Purdy's*
– Courtesy Jim Maunder

In the late 1930s electricity was available on Penlake. What a difference that made to daily living! No more lamps to clean every morning, no wicks to trim, no fire to fear. Better lighting made the evenings enjoyable for reading, writing, and entertaining, too. As outdoor lighting illuminated the cottages, the lake became "alive" at night, as well as by day. Electrical devices such as stoves, heaters, various kitchen gadgets, water pumps, and refrigerators made daily chores easier. Eventually even dishwashers were introduced.

Faster boats became popular. The outboard replaced the dispro, and distant shores were more accessible. The lake became a united community.

The telephone also had a major effect on daily life. Messages no longer had to be hand-delivered. A phone call enabled residents to order supplies from Huntsville and to communicate with other cottagers.

Many cottages on Penlake today are winterized and enjoyed year-round. With the advances in building materials and techniques, construction has much improved. Cottages are considerably more animal-proof, and easier to heat and keep clean. Penlakers have become environmentally conscious now, too. Garbage is no longer burned, but taken to the dump. Septic systems have been inspected and most upgraded to government specifications. Care is taken of the lake, and water quality has become everyone's concern.

*AMD*

*Grandmother Reid and the* Ramona
– Courtesy T.L. Moffat IV

# THE ALGONQUIN

*Meeting the* Algonquin *by skiff.*
– Courtesy Dorothy Mansell Eastmure

**Huntsville and Lake of Bays Line**

## SUMMER TIME TABLE 1952
IN EFFECT JUNE 28th AND UNTIL FURTHER NOTICE AND UNLESS OTHERWISE STATED

**Huntsville - Portage - Dorset**

| | | | | RAILWAY SERVICE — EASTERN STANDARD TIME | | | | | |
|---|---|---|---|---|---|---|---|---|---|
| x | 11.30 p.m. | B | 8.45 a.m. | Lve. | Toronto, via C.N. Rys. | Arr. | D | 7.05 p.m. | X | 7.10 a.m. |
| x | 4.18 a.m. | B | 12.53 p.m. | Arr. | Huntsville Station | Lve. | D | 1.32 p.m. | X | 1.45 a.m. |

| FROM HUNTSVILLE READ DOWN | | | | STEAMER SERVICE — EASTERN DAYLIGHT SAVING TIME | | FROM DORSET READ UP | | |
|---|---|---|---|---|---|---|---|---|
| D | 9.00 a.m. | D | 3.00 p.m. | Lve. | Huntsville (Town Wharf) | Arr. | D | 12.25 p.m. | D | 6.40 p.m. |
| A | 9.30 a.m. | A | | Arr. | Swallowdale | Arr. | A | | A | |
| A | 9.35 a.m. | A | | Arr. | Grandview (Fairy Lake) | Arr. | A | | A | |
| A | | A | | Arr. | Canal | Arr. | A | | A | |
| A | 9.55 a.m. | A | | Arr. | Pow Wow Point | Arr. | T | | A | |
| A | 10.00 a.m. | A | | Arr. | Grassmere (Tally Ho) | | | A | |
| A | 10.10 a.m. | T | | Arr. | Isle Dunelg | Arr. | T | | A | |
| A | | A | | Arr. | Sekani | Arr. | A | | A | |
| A | 10.15 a.m. | A | | Arr. | Springsyde | Arr. | T | | A | |
| D | 10.20 a.m. | D | 4.00 p.m. | Arr. | North Portage | Lve. | D | 11.15 a.m. | D | 5.10 p.m. |
| D | 11.00 a.m. | D | 5.00 p.m. | Lve. | South Portage | Arr. | D | 10.40 a.m. | A | 4.25 p.m. |
| A | 11.10 a.m. | D | 5.10 p.m. | Arr. | Britannia | Lve. | D | 10.30 a.m. | A | 4.15 p.m. |
| A | 11.50 a.m. | A | 5.50 p.m. | Arr. | Bona Vista | Lve. | A | | A | |
| A | 12.00 a.m. | A | 6.00 p.m. | Arr. | Point Ideal | Lve. | A | | A | |
| A | | A | | Arr. | Robinsdale | Lve. | A | | A | |
| A | 12.10 a.m. | A | 6.10 p.m. | Arr. | Glenmount | Lve. | A | 9.15 a.m. | A | 3.15 p.m. |
| D | 12.30 a.m. | D | 6.30 p.m. | Arr. | Bigwin Island (Bigwin Inn) | Lve. | D | 9.00 a.m. | A | 3.00 p.m. |
| A | 12.40 a.m. | A | | Arr. | Port Cunnington | Lve. | A | | A | |
| A | | A | | Arr. | Grove Park Lodge | Lve. | A | | A | |
| A | | A | | Arr. | Chevaliers | Lve. | A | | A | |
| A | | A | | Arr. | Cliffdene | Lve. | A | | D | |
| A | | A | | Arr. | Raymor Pines | Lve. | A | | A | |
| D | 1.00 p.m. | D | 7.10 p.m. | Arr. | Dorset | Lve. | D | 8.00 a.m. | A | 2.15 p.m. |

### Explanation of Signs

X—Daily.      D—Daily except Sunday.      B—Friday and Saturday only.

T—Call will only be made to take on or deliver passengers, to or from trains.

A—Steamers will stop to land any passengers, and will pick up on previous arrangement.
Flag Signals—The Company will not under any circumstances accept responsibility for failure to stop on flag call. Where steamers are required to call at wharves (designated A) for outgoing passengers, General Offices must be notified 24 hours previous or the Captain of the Steamer 12 hours previous in writing.

Time table shows steamers should arrive at and leave different ports, but their departure, arrival or connection at time stated is not guaranteed nor does the Company hold itself responsible for any delays or any consequences arising therefrom or for failure on the part of steamers to call by appointment or notice, either verbal or written, at any regular stopping places. All times subject to fluctuation from stress of weather, etc., and change with or without notice.

**C. R. McLennan,**
President and Gen. Mgr.
Huntsville, Ont., June 28th, 1952

**W. J. Moore,**
Vice-Pres. and Sec.-Treas.

*Algonquin and train timetable from 1952*
– Courtesy Anna Mirrette Darling

WHEN THE CANAL from Fairy Lake to Peninsula Lake was completed in 1888, water transportation was provided by privately owned steamers and tugs. Some of the early steamers, such as the *Excelsior, Empress Victoria,* and the *Joe,* plied Penlake until 1906. In that year the *Algonquin* was built at South Portage, hauled across to North Portage — breaking her "back" in the process — and pressed into regular service between Huntsville and North Portage. The only time service was cut off was in 1926, when she was rebuilt after catching fire in Lake Vernon.

The early steamers transported freight and passengers, but the *Algonquin* played a far more important role for the summer residents on Penlake: she became a focal point for a way of life. Her steady progress around the lake to the familiar resorts was followed with great interest and speculation as to why she was going into Winoka, the Isle Dunelg, Put-in-Bay, Springsyde, and on rare occasions down into Hill's Bay. By the time she reached the island, she was often accompanied by all sorts of watercraft: classic launches, dispros, a few skiffs, and in later years, little outboards.

Most of these small craft headed directly to the Portage to greet the *Algonquin* on arrival, but many stayed with her, buzzing around like flies, playing in her wake and showing off to the passengers, all the while driving the poor *Algonquin* captain to distraction. On one occasion R.H. Henderson took his wife out in Fred Henderson's sea flea, leaving the children on the dock as he darted about the *Algonquin.* To the horror of all, his little craft promptly flipped as it went over the huge wake. Fortunately no one was hurt.

On the *Algonquin* 's morning run, the most important cargo was the mail. The mailbag was hustled up to the Portage store and post office where Bill Hood — or Blake Walton, Alice Thompson, Sam Manning — waited to sort the mail. The postmaster was always surrounded by a small horde of teenagers from around the lake who, while they awaited their deliveries, chatted and made plans for the coming day or evening.

The outgoing mail, bagged and hauled down to the Portage Wharf, was literally tossed on board the *Algonquin* for the trip to Huntsville. On one occasion the bag missed the boat and landed in the water. A great scurry ensued and the mailbag was rescued, luckily none the worse for the experience.

The afternoon run presented a slightly different scene, for the main attraction was the throng of tourists who had come up on the afternoon train. The hustle and bustle and excitement were often capped by teenagers showing off their diving prowess from the top deck of the *Algonquin* to the applause of the assembled spectators and the shouted threats of the frustrated captain.

The captain of the *Algonquin* was a navigator without peer. How he managed to steer a course through the lakes, let alone the twists and turns of the narrow

*Gathering cord wood for the* Algonquin.
– Courtesy Don Marshall

*The* Algonquin *in the canal. Note cord wood*
*for fuel stacked along the shore.*
– Courtesy Agnes Moffat McGee

*The* Iroquois II *passing the Marshall boathouse.*
– Courtesy Don Marshall

canal in dense fog, has always been a point of admiration and wonder for me. Once, Ian Eastmure and I went to Huntsville in a small outboard to attend the late movie. We were dismayed to find that at the end of the movie the fog was so thick that returning to Penlake was impossible. Undaunted, we spent the rest of the night sleeping in the passenger lounge of the *Algonquin*. The morning was still shrouded in fog. Unbeknownst to anyone on board, we made fast to the stern and enjoyed a comfortable trip, pulled into the safety and security of Penlake before being discovered and unceremoniously set adrift. Fortunately the fog had begun to burn off.

Because the canal was so twisting and narrow, the captain would always blow his whistle before entering it, and the prudent boater would patiently wait until the steamer had navigated the canal before entering it. One day, however, Bill Blackburn was hauling a small log boom through the canal with the Blackburn motor launch, *Put-in-Bay*. The boom became stuck and poor Bill had to leave it behind and race out to Fairy Lake to warn the captain of the problem. The boom was eventually unstuck and its journey through the canal completed, but not before the *Algonquin* had spent some time making numerous circles around Fairy Lake.

The steamboats lent a unique quality to life at Penlake, drawing the residents together into a very special sort of community. The retirement of the *Algonquin* in 1952 heralded a new era, which sadly will never recapture the romance of the past.

*RDM*

# THE PORTAGE FLYER

Y OU COULD HEAR ITS WHISTLE — shrill and loud — and the sound made your heart pound a little faster. You could see the billowing smoke marking its passage as it chugged through the woods on its short run.

"The Little Train is coming!" Penlake cottagers could mark the time of day by the cry of a youngster racing to the dock for the day's first sighting of this local phenomenon. The *Portage Flyer*, "the smallest commercially operated railway in the world," ran on narrow-gauge rails laid between South Portage on Lake of Bays and North Portage on Peninsula Lake.

In the late 1800s a series of locks were built, opening up a water route from Port Sydney on Mary Lake to Huntsville. Already a steamboat plied regularly between those ports. A canal had also been dug between Fairy and Peninsula lakes, thus providing an additional steamer route.

Another canal had been proposed to link Lake of Bays, to the south, and Peninsula Lake, to the north. The idea was abandoned when it became apparent that two sets of locks would be required in the short canal to accommodate the hundred-foot difference in height between the lakes. The cost of such a project was deemed prohibitive. Instead, in 1887 a sturdy gravel road was built between the portages.

As transportation improved, the area became a mecca for tourists. Hotels sprang up and flourished. Many guests fell in love with the area and became landowners and cottagers. Train service from Toronto and other points south was regular. The demand for reliable transportation to specific destinations saw the creation of the Huntsville and Lake of Bays Navigation Company. Large and small steamboats with names like *Mohawk Bell, Algonquin, Ramona,* and *Iroquois* were brought into service.

The most logical means to get passengers from Lake of Bays to Peninsula Lake and vice versa was by train. To reflect this reality, the Navigation Company changed its name in 1903 to the Huntsville & Lake of Bays Railroad Company. Construction began on rail beds to carry a small train back and forth between the lakes.

In his book *By Steam Boat and By Steam Train*, Huntsville historian Niall MacKay vividly describes the genesis of the *Portage Flyer* from the formation of the Navigation Company and the actual layout of the rail bed to the purchase of the "two 1888 vintage H.K. Porter 0-4-0 saddle tank locomotives."

The two open-air passenger cars were actually old streetcars. The smaller one was a fifty-seat ex-Toronto suburban railway car built by the Toronto Railway Company. The larger car, a seventy-five seater built by Jackson and Sharp, came to Penlake from Atlantic City, New Jersey, part of that city's trolley system.

In addition to the difference in height between Lake of Bays and Peninsula Lake, the topography of the land includes a sizable ridge, thereby increasing the

*Portage Flyer souvenir ticket*
– Courtesy Evelyn Walton Kimmel Taylor

*A Portage Flyer postcard from 1928*
– Courtesy Anna Mirrette Darling

*Passenger exchange at the Portage*
– Courtesy Irwin Schultz

*The* Portage Flyer *at North Portage, with the Wawaneika boathouse in background. This Porter steam engine was nicknamed "the boiling tea kettle."*
– Courtesy Dorothy Mansell Eastmure and Bob Moffat

lift between the lakes. It was not unheard of, when the Little Train was running fully loaded with freight and passengers, for a few stalwarts to disembark and give the train a bit of help "over the hump."

By the late 1940s the *Portage Flyer* was, in fact, over the hill; its boilers were declared unsafe to operate. Two other locomotives, originally owned by the Canadian Gypsum Company, were purchased through a railroad supplier in Toronto and were shipped from Nova Scotia to Toronto to be adapted for use between the portages. When the new season arrived, engine number five was pressed into service and pulled the Little Train from the summer of 1948 until its final run in the late 1950s.

With the improved roads, the automobile became the usual mode of transportation to the cottages and hotels. The *Portage Flyer* passed its last years mainly as a tourist attraction. After the retirement of the *Algonquin* in 1952, a smaller boat, the *Iroquois II*, was pressed into service to bring tourists out from Huntsville to enjoy a ride on the world-famous train. In 1959, the year after the *Iroquois II* stopped running, the *Portage Flyer* made its last run.

Longtime Penlakers well remember the Little Train and may even recall sneaking a ride on one of the boxcars. Waiting stealthily in the woods near the switchback, many a youngster waited for just the right moment to hop aboard the car when the train slowed to a near stop to reverse its engine. The engineers pretended not to notice, for hitching a ride on the Little Train was a rite of summer.

*ISA*

# POST OFFICES

For NEARLY A CENTURY SEVERAL POST OFFICES met the needs of the widely scattered rural communities that dotted the landscape near Peninsula Lake. The townships of Chaffey and Sinclair were served by the Grassmere Post Office, while Franklin had post offices at Hillside and North Portage.

In addition to providing postal services, these post offices were community centres where neighbours met, friendships grew, gossip was shared, and plans were made. This was particularly true during the summer when the population swelled with the arrival of the cottagers.

By the mid-1980s no post offices serving Penlake remained, although rural mail delivery is still available in certain areas. The nearest post offices are in Dwight and Huntsville.

## GRASSMERE POST OFFICE

Robert Ballantine opened the Grassmere Post Office in his home in 1874. It served Chaffey and Sinclair townships in the District of Muskoka until its closing in 1957. Records from the Canada Post Museum show that in its first year of operation the Grassmere Post Office paid Mr. Ballantine $3.33 and made a profit of $1.38. Other postmasters, their names found in the postal archives, are as follows:

| | |
|---|---|
| 1874-1892 | ROBERT BALLANTYNE |
| 1893-1921 | MRS. MARY M. BALLANTYNE |
| 1921-1931 | MRS. MARY FIELD |
| 1931-1951 | MRS. MARY OKE |
| 1951-1957 | KENNETH RALPH BALLANTYNE |

## HILLSIDE POST OFFICE

The HILLSIDE POST OFFICE first opened in November 1878, but was closed in January 1879. Rev. Robert Norton Hill was the first postmaster.

The post office reopened in 1898 in the Hodgson home. Six separate locations for the Hillside Post Office are recorded. Those who have served as postmasters/mistresses at Hillside are as follows:

| | | |
|---|---|---|
| Nov. 1878-Jan. 1879 | REV. R.N. HILL | (office at home) |
| 1898-1905 | ALBERT HODGSON | (office at home) |
| 1905-1926 | T. ROWLAND HILL | (office at home) |
| 1927 | FRANK MILLAR | (office at home) |
| 1928-1937 | DOROTHY McQUIRTER | (office at home) |
| 1938-1943 | VIOLET HILL | (office in Maplewood) |
| 1943-1945 | MARY TAPLEY | (office in Maplewood) |
| 1946-1969 | GRACE PETERSEN | (office in Maplewood) |

From 1963 until its closing in 1969, the Hillside Post Office provided service during the summer months only.

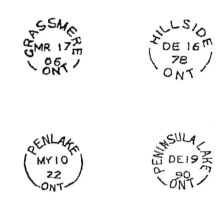

*Grassmere Post Office*
– Drawing by Dibbie Spurr Appleton

# PENLAKE POST OFFICE

*Top: Dorothy Eastmure
at the Penlake Post Office.*
– Photo by Marion Cobban
*Bottom:"No more mail."
The Hillside Post Office
building as it looked in 1993.*
– Photo by Mrs. Norman Moffat

THE CANADA POST ARCHIVES indicate that as early as 1890 a post office designated Peninsula Lake was opened at South Portage. The postmaster was John G. Henderson. This post office closed in 1903, but was reopened on the same site on August 27, 1904, and renamed Portage. Louis Keown was the first postmaster.

The minutes of the Springsyde Cottagers' Association dated August 31, 1921, read: "It was moved by Mr. Cherrier, seconded by Miss Fasken, that the directors take the necessary steps to secure for next season, a summer post office at North Portage. Approved. It was proposed that Mr. Hood, if willing, should be the Post Master and that the office be called Peninsula Lake or some other suitable name."

And so the Penlake Post Office was opened at North Portage as a summer operation on June 1, 1922. Its business was carried out in the North Portage store.

"Going to Portage" was a familiar cry on Penlake for many years. And little wonder, for as well as offering full postal services, the store carried a variety of groceries; there was a gas pump at the dock, and the wharf served as a terminus for the *Algonquin* and other boats; the tracks for the *Portage Flyer* ended at the dock, facilitating the journey to South Portage and Lake of Bays; and for cottagers without phone service, a public phone was available.

The Canada Post Archives contains the following list of postmasters for the Penlake Post Office:

| | |
|---|---|
| 1922-1941 | WILLIAM NOLAN HOOD |
| 1941-1944 | EDWARD BLAKE WALTON |
| 1945-1948 | JOHN ALEXANDER THOMPSON |
| 1948-1959 | SAMUEL EDGE MANNING |
| 1960-1965 | MRS. ALICE LILLIAN MANNING |
| 1965- | GORDON EDWARD FLETCHER |

Sadly for the cottagers, the Penlake Post Office was closed in 1977.

*ISA*

# NORTH PORTAGE STORE

THE AREA AROUND THE PORTAGE was Crown land granted to Hugh Taylor in 1883. In 1910 Eleanor Hood purchased part of one acre, which was to become the North
Portage Store. In 1919 her husband, William Hood, acquired the entire parcel of land and the store.

In 1941 the Hoods sold the store to May Evelyn Walton. According to Evie Walton Kimmel Taylor, "The first
time we arrived in May to open the store my mother was
so badly bitten by black flies that she had to wrap her
legs." The store came with a handful of cottages and one
very small cabin perched on the rock overlooking the
wharf. This cabin, named Whip Inn, was rented to young
friends of the family who were working in the area for the
summer.

The store was a fully stocked grocery. Staples were
delivered by truck; fresh vegetables and meats were ordered by phone from Huntsville and picked up the next day
by Evie. The porch was screened in and filled with tables
and chairs, which made it a favourite place to enjoy ice
cream or a cold drink while waiting for the mail to be sorted. Evie remembers Rev. David Marshall coming each day
from nearby Fisher's Point with his Irish setter. He would
purchase an ice-cream cone for his dog, who would sit and
lick it!

In 1941 the Waltons sold the store to Alex and Alice
Thompson, who ran it successfully until it was purchased
by Mr. and Mrs. Manning in 1948. Sixteen years later the
Mannings sold to Gordon E. Fletcher and his wife, Edna
Dorothy. In 1978 the Fletchers moved to South Portage,
selling to Jack Martin English and his wife, Margaret Jean.

In 1983 Freddy and Sientge Ruisendaal bought the
property and ran a smaller convenience store from the converted boathouse; they also did work for cottagers along
the shore. The following year, they sold a half interest to
Bob and Rick Evers. In 1989 these two parties sold the
property to North Portage Hideaway Inc. There are now
two very large, beautifully designed duplexes on the site.

*Evie Walton Kimmel Taylor and DME*

*Waiting for a boat at North Portage in 1914.*

**FIRE! The bucket brigade battles the blaze that destroyed the
historic Portage Hotel and wharf buildings in the early 1900s.**

– Photos courtesy Irwin Schultz

79

# AIRPLANES

IN THE MID-1920S bush pilots came to Peninsula Lake, landing their planes by the beach at Tally Ho. Guests at the inn and cottagers on the lake could take ten-minute flights over the area, and because airplanes were unique and flights rare, it was a real adventure. But a flight did cost five dollars!

A few years later, during the era when Mom and the kids came for the entire summer and Dad joined them only on weekends and on his vacation time, the seaplane was the transport of choice for many men. I can recall my uncle, George Foster, arriving early one morning from Pittsburgh. A stop at the Canadian border had been required, and the customs official had accepted the pilot's invitation to fly up to the cottage with them and afterward return to the border with the pilot.

Several individuals had their own planes. I can remember the Hubble plane taking off for Huntsville every morning and returning just before sunset. It was rather frightening to be out in a small boat when the plane was descending direct-ly overhead. Today the beautiful airplane belonging to Orville Wright is a well-recognized feature along the shore across from Deerhurst, as is Doug Woollings's plane in Grassmere Bay.

*AMD*

# ICE CUTTING

ICE IN THE LAKE could be either a curse or a blessing. If there was a strong onshore wind in the spring when the ice was going out, it could be a curse, as evi-denced by the many devastated docks and boathouses along the shores.

Deep in the winter months the ice was a blessing, particularly if it was two or three feet thick. Blocks of ice could be cut to provision the numerous icehouses around the lake. Large ice saws, either mechanically driven or powered by the sweat of the brow, were used to make large sections of the lake into enormous ice cubes. These were hauled in horse-drawn sleighs to shore, where they were packed in a bed of sawdust and stored in icehouses for use during the summer months.

The lake, however, presented considerable hazard before the ice holes refroze. On one occasion a colt heard its mother's whinny — she had been harnessed to pull blocks of ice from the lake. The hapless young horse raced from the barn, across a field, and onto the ice. As he scrambled across the treacherous surface, the colt did not see the large expanse of open water between him and his mother. He skidded into the abyss, went under the ice, and could not be saved.

Fortunately for the many snowmobilers zooming around the lake today, ice cutting is no longer necessary. Although, on second thought...

*RDM*

# OUTHOUSES

It was the summer of 1991. Indy Jarrett rose to the occasion. Standing somberly before the serious group, he waited for quiet, then eloquently delivered the verse quoted on the right.

The occasion was the naming of an outhouse. Built by the new owners of Windstone cottage, it met all the government standards. Guests came with homemade bathroom accessories and offered such likely names as Par Two, Two Can (it was a two-holer), and Thunder Bay. L'il Windy drew on the cottage name, but the judges' consensus fell to Windsthrone.

For early cottagers, outhouses were essential. Later, as more and more cottages were fitted with indoor plumbing, many an owner kept his outhouse in good repair as a backup, or for occasions when there was an overflow — of guests, that is!

Outhouses came with names like Bear House, Over the Hill, and Up the Hill — because they usually were. There was also the Throne Room, the Reading Room, the Dapper Crapper, and at one cottage where poker was a popular pastime, the owners might well have called their completely plumbed outhouse Royal Flush.

Most outhouses were strictly utilitarian, but one or two verged on palatial. The William Penn at the McCreadys' was a splendid three-hole affair named for a Pittsburgh hotel. Sporting lace curtains at its doorway, it even offered the joys of fine music — from a music box connected to the toilet-paper dispenser!

Many families demolishing old outhouses have come upon hidden treasures. Caches of whisky bottles buried in very rich soil tell the tale of teenagers who discovered the sins of their elders. And if cigarette wrappings weren't mostly biodegradable, doubtless a few interesting stories could be told there. When you get to the bottom of it, the old outhouse is a source of all sorts of weird and wonderful tales!

*ISA*

*There was a young man named Hyde*
*Who fell down a privy and died.*
*Then his brother*
*Fell down another,*
*And now they're interred side by side.*

*Anonymous*

*from* The Lure of the Limerick
*by Arthur Sullivan*
– Photo courtesy Whitney Holloway

*One of Professor Laing's fishing parties, circa 1912. Left to right: ?, Professor Laing, Mr. Whyte,*
*Perce Mansell, Wm. Mansell; the young boy is Jack Moffat (the Reverend ...one day).*
– Courtesy T.L. Moffat IV

# RECREATION

## FISHING

**M**ANY EARLY COTTAGERS were attracted to Peninsula Lake because of its plentiful supply of fish — particularly bass and trout, which were a welcome addition to the daily fare.

Others simply enjoyed the sport, although their families also got to enjoy the spoils. My father, Arch Campbell, used to rise before dawn and be out fishing by six, usually with Joe Bullen or Howard De Van. They had their favourite spots: Hill's Bay and Winoka Reef. If they were going after trout, they fished from Casselman's Point to the Birches, the deepest part of the lake, requiring many feet of copper line.

In the early 1920s, if you caught any large fish, you took them to be weighed at Deerhurst. The inn presented an annual trophy for the largest fish caught in the lake. My father won the trophy several times until the inn declared that the trophy was for guests only.

Jack Hodgins was another ardent fisherman. He usually caught big lake trout by trolling in the early spring. His fishing buddies were Roy and Hartley Henderson, and Fred Silvester, who was particularly fond of fishing at Winoka.

Mary and Bill Weaber were also keen fishermen. Even before they bought their cottage, they purchased a launch, which they named *Mary,* for fishing forays.

Dougal Cameron helped perpetuate the love of fishing. He used to take the young boys on Springsyde out fishing every morning at the crack of dawn, and he would pass his special fishing secrets on to them.

Every shore — Springsyde, Wolf Bay, and Hill's Bay — had its fishermen, who all had their special spots and their favourite times and their preferred weather conditions.

Probably the most enthusiastic fisherman on Penlake was Claude Musselman, for whom fishing was a passion. The following pictures speak for themselves.

*AMD*

*"Hold it up higher!" - 1925;*
*a 6½-pound smallmouth bass held*
*by Anna Mirrette Campbell.*
– Courtesy Anna Mirrette Darling

*"We caught it!" - 1968;*
*David Kennard and Don McIntosh.*
– Courtesy David Kennard

# Memories of Fishing

*Right: Agnes Moffat McGee with the catch of the day.*
– Courtesy Agnes Moffat McGee

*Far right: Claude Musselman with his son George in 1945.*
– Courtesy the Musselman family

*Bottom: A day's catch at Windstone; left to right: L.D. Brown, Margaret and Crawford Brown, Mrs. Ogle, and Nell Brown, 1915.*
– Courtesy the Spurr family

*Bottom right: "Mine's bigger!" Left to right: Frances, Gordon, and Olive Moffat, 1925.*
– Courtesy Bob Moffat

# GOLFING

*Four of the Hendersons golfing at the links.*
– Courtesy Ted Harper

THE GOLF COURSE was the inspiration of Gene Henderson, a passionate golfer. In 1912 he bought the point of land stretching from Hill's Bay toward Hill's Island — the Pea Field, which was originally part of Rev. Hill's Crown grant. With some professional help, he had the course laid out. As he was a southpaw, the course favoured left-handers. He called it Guernsey Woods Golf Club.

A cabin served as a small office, snack shop, and caddy house. After the gentlemen finished their round, they gathered there to determine their winnings, for all sorts of bets and side bets had been made. They could be heard for hours calculating, "One up, even, one down, two down..." until all matches were settled. There were also a good number of ladies who enjoyed special field days, monthly tournaments, and masquerades.

The golf course became a social centre for the cottage community. During the First World War, what had been the ninth hole was plowed to make a "victory garden." In the early 1920s Gene Henderson built a large screened pavilion in the woods near the sixth tee, where a few trees were encircled with wooden benches. One winter, a few years later, at was moved closer to the lakeshore.

During nondenominational Sunday church services, guest singers were invited to perform, including Ida Dilworth and the incomparable soprano Lois Marshall.

On Saturday nights the pavilion became a dance hall, hosting square dances, concerts, children's masquerades, and other festivities. In the 1950s and 1960s buffet dinners and corn roasts were held there, and on the evening following the annual regatta people danced to the strains of a live orchestra.

In the summer of 1929 it was rumoured that Gene Henderson's health was

*Laying out the golf course.*
*Left to right: Dr. Richardson,*
*Tom Stevens, Fred McEwen,*
*Mr. Ogle (in the straw hat), ?,*
*Mr. Dilworth, Fred Henderson,*
*G.E. Henderson, and*
*Freeman Ogle, circa 1913.*
– Courtesy Nancy
Henderson Smart

failing and that his second wife, May, wanted to turn the golf course into a boys' camp. Horrified, four golfers formed a partnership to buy the course: Dr. James McCready, his brother-in-law Ed Brown, and Howard De Van all from Pittsburgh, Pennsylvania, joined forces with, Archie Campbell from Toronto.

These four had great plans for the course, now called Penlake Farms Golf Club, which they promptly put into action. Watering systems were installed at all the greens. Number-nine hole became number one. A high tee was constructed so that those putting on the green could be seen from the tee. This was called Camel's Hump, a play on the way the Americans pronounced Campbell. The new number-four tee was moved back into the woods to lengthen the hole. This was named Bachelor's Retreat for Ed Brown. Number-six hole had an overhanging limb of an elm, which Dr. McCready viewed as a hazard to his drives. This hole was therefore Doctor's Limb. Since Howard De Van was in the investment business and an accurate player, he often scored on number nine, with his drive being closest to the hole; hence number nine was Broker's Paradise.

In the mid-1920s Gene Henderson built a cottage near the new first hole. This cottage eventually became the clubhouse and was the prime reason for renumbering the holes. The sleeping cabins made useful equipment buildings — except for the one that became the junior clubhouse, managed by Emily Jean McCready, Virginia Springer, Jane De Van, and Anna Mirrette Campbell, who had an average age of eight! The girls held bake sales for the *Toronto Star* Fresh Air Fund. Parents donated supplies from the tuck shop, and Mrs. Hinton, the store- and bookkeeper, made delicious orange juice. Most of the goodies were resold at inflated prices to parents!

The big clubhouse was furnished by donations. The McCreadys sent up old wicker furniture as "settlers' effects," which a coat of bright paint and newly upholstered cushions utterly transformed. Ava McCready painted rockers green with large roses; other chairs were painted yellow and orange and reupholstered in striking prints; orange curtain rods were hung with orange, yellow, and black-striped fabric; green carpeting was laid. Gifts of pictures, lamps, tables, a yellow mission oak desk, a large wind-up gramophone, dishes, cutlery, and glasses came from many sources.

By the 1930s the clubhouse was the showplace of the lake and the centre of many activities — from the Penlake Association annual meetings to the ladies' social membership parties; potluck luncheons; bridge and afternoon tea; and Sunday-evening buffet suppers with Howard De Van and Arch Campbell sporting tall white chef's hats and doing the carving.

It held the annual luncheon for the ladies' golf awards ceremony, too, and displayed the championship plaques, the handicap trophies, and the CLGU score and handicap sheets. Fran Cox provided cocktails before the luncheon. Tournaments often had more than thirty entries. There would be a championship flight, consolation, and first and second flight. Eula Campbell, Ann De Van, Ida Dilworth, Sylvia Dilworth, Eleanor Foster, Marg Spurr, Fran Cox, and her daughter Dorothy Wyndham were among the top players.

There was also the men's championship, which was based on allotted handicaps and for which a cup was presented. This was a very popular tournament, many of the golfers arranging their holidays so that they could compete in this week-long elimination event.

But one winter in the 1970s, unnoticed for a month or so, the clubhouse mysteriously burned to the ground. Everything was lost except the stone fireplace. When the pavilion was demolished in 1988, Rob and Cathy Hurst retrieved the hardwood flooring for the home they later built on the site. Many old-timers now cherish the old church benches and pews, salvaged through the generosity of Bill McCready and Emily Sieber.

Penlake Farms Golf Course contributed to the local economy. The course required two maintenance men from early spring to late fall. Mike Hinton was the foreman from 1929 until his untimely death in the late 1930s. His assistant, George McQuirter, carried on into the 1960s. They were followed by a series of groundskeepers, some for only a season, others, like Sam Wright, for many years. The store- and bookkeeping required considerable help also. Aileen Hinton was the first to hold this position, setting the standard for those who followed, including Mrs. Blake Hill and Mrs. Elsie Campbell.

Caddies played a big part in the early days. Junior cottagers from around Penlake spent some of their summer caddying. The local children relied heavily on the earnings from caddying, especially during the Great Depression. Many

*Lady golfers at Guernsey Woods – 1927-1928. Left to right: Gladys Smale, Eula Campbell, Lillian Smale, Isobel Smale, Ava McCready, May Henderson, Izzer Hutcheson, Jean McCready, Mabel Best, Ann DeVan, Fannie Cox, and Anna Mirrette Campbell in front.*

*The Star Fresh Air Fund helpers. Back row, left to right: Bill Hodgins, Ted Harper, and Hartley Henderson. Front row, left to right: Nancy Henderson, Emily Jean McCready, Anne Mirrette Campbell, Virgie Springer, and Mildred Jones.*

*Gentlemen golfers at the golf course. Left to right: Dr. J.H. (Puddy) McCready, Arch Campbell, George Johnstone, G.E. Henderson, and Clint Spurr.*
– Photos courtesy Anna Mirrette Darling

*Gentlemen golfers. Left to right: Howard DeVan, R.J. Dilworth, ?, ?, G.E. Henderson, Arch Campbell, George Johnstone, Bill Smale, Dr. J.H. McCready, Jim McCready, Fred McEwen, Bill Brown, Max Wyndham, ? . Sitting in front are Dorothy Wyndham, Nell Wooldridge, Ada Dobson, Ann DeVan, and Ava McCready.*

– Courtesy Anna Mirrette Darling

walked or rode their bikes from considerable distances, brought their lunch, and hoped to get at least one job a day, though some were awfully small to be carrying such heavy bags. A few lucky ones caddied regularly for particular golfers.

When the golf course was purchased in 1929, the partners wanted to secure a right-of-way road into the property. They purchased land between the township road and the golf course from Gordon Hill of Limberlost. Hill would only sell his entire holding, which included four lakefront lots — purchased later by Dr. William Weaber, Dr. George Vance Foster, and Anna Mirrette (Campbell) Darling — and the woods and field to the south of the township road almost to Highway 60 (now owned by Mr. Holmes).

In 1940 Campbell and De Van sold their interests in the golf course to Jean McCready. Upon the death of her brother, Ed Brown, she inherited his share and after Dr. McCready died, she controlled the entire golf course. After her death her children, Emily Sieber and Bill McCready, became joint owners.

Over the years season members, male or female, were fewer and fewer. Summer vacations were shortening from all summer to two weeks and weekends. Many

*The ladies' tea at the golf course clubhouse in 1931.*
– Courtesy Emily McCready Sieber

*Golf tournament – 1940s. Left to right:*
*Dick Alcorn, Jimmy Hardie, Clint Spurr, ?, Jean Jarrett, Norm Hill, ?, Gish Foster (Scully), Homer Jarrett, Marjorie Jarrett, Fred Cruickshank, Charles Jarrett, Don Cruickshank. Seated: Emmy McCready (Sieber), Donnie Hill, and ?.*
– Courtesy the Spurr family

younger people were turning to tennis and did not spend as much time at Penlake as their parents had. The nearby Deerhurst Golf Course and the improvement of other courses in the area provided stiff competition for membership. Even the number of daily players dwindled. Penlake Farms had never been a money-making venture and in 1988 the land was subdivided and put up for sale.

The road now meets township standards. All the lots on the course have been sold, and much of the wooded area has been bought by cottagers along the lakeshore to increase their property and ensure themselves against infringing development. And no doubt at some future date someone will ask, "Why is it called the Golf Course Road?"

*AMD*

## LYLE NELSON'S HOLE IN ONE

Dr. Lyle Nelson was one of the finest golfers to grace the Penlake Farms course. Unfortunately he tended to be too trusting of friends and colleagues.

One sunny July morning in the late 1940s, while playing with John Hay, Bill Weaber, and George Foster, Lyle got a hole in one on the difficult par-three sixth hole, a 160-yard challenge into the prevailing wind with several storeys in height of elm, maple, and fir protecting the green from anything except a fade or a pitch and run. At the end of the round the foursome repaired to George Foster's cottage, Hie Away, to celebrate Lyle's achievement.

At first, with customary Missourian modesty, Lyle protested that it was just a lucky shot. Then, as more drinks were consumed, he began to agree with his three fellow physicians, who had acted like adoring acolytes, that he was indeed an exceptional golfer. Finally the question was popped: "Well, do you think you could do it again?"

Probably beyond the thinking stage, Lyle replied, "Of course I can."

"I'll bet you can't," one of them challenged.

The result was $100 even money from each of them against five hundred tries at the hole-in-one from the middle of the sixth tee the next afternoon. Of course, they could have given him a thousand tries, or even two thousand, because after just 115 shots — one of which actually bounced into the pin — Lyle's arms were too tired even to hold a drink, let alone a five iron. He paid up.

To their credit, the wives of Drs. Foster and Weaber said they should give the money back. Irene Nelson was furious that her husband's buddies had taken such advantage of him. Under pressure, a weak offer to cancel was made from the trio of physician/con artists. Lyle, a true gentleman, refused. He even warned that he would get his money back. As the most consistent and accomplished golfer, he likely did, many times over.

*Briar Foster*

*Top: Bill McCready presents a golf trophy to Bill McEwen.*
– Courtesy Bill McCready
*Middle: Bill McCready presents a golf trophy to Lee Cook, circa 1960.*
– Courtesy the Spurr family
*Bottom: Dr. John Hay presents the winner's trophy to Ellen McEwen.*
– Courtesy Bill McCready

*The* Glasgow, *one of the earliest launches on the lake, circa 1907.*
*Owned jointly by J.K., T.L. and F.W. Moffat, the* Glasgow *is shown here with J.K. Moffat*
*standing in the bow, and Scottish ensign flying in the background.*
– Courtesy Bob Moffat

# BOATS ON PENLAKE

In the early days, boats were essential for transportation, as few cottages had road access. Although gasoline was relatively expensive, people used their boats frequently. It was common to go boating as a family. If a family did not have a boat, they often joined one who did.

In the early 1900s the choice of boats was limited. Canoes included the popular Sponson, or "safety" canoe, which could be paddled or rowed. It served equally well for transportation and recreation. Everyone had a rowboat and rowed as a matter of course. Some boats were innovative, ranging from the family washtub to the more sophisticated raft.

Powerboats were rare at the turn of the century. The earliest were steamboats converted to gasoline-powered engines. Hulls tended to be white, and cockpits were large and usually lined with benches. Engines, too, were large and exposed at midship.

As the gasoline engine became more advanced, so did boat design. With the engines mounted forward of the main cockpit, the bow section was invariably half the boat's length with a knife-like prow that sliced through the water. There was room in the cockpit now for wicker chairs, many of which grace cottage verandahs today. These boats were popular from the First World War through to the early 1930s.

At about the same time the popular disappearing-propeller boats — DPs or dispros — made their appearance. They weren't fast, but they were seaworthy and could take a great cargo of goods or people.

*The DP, also known as the Disappearing Propeller, the Dispro, and the Dippy. The DP was particularly popular after the First World War and into the 1930s.*
– Courtesy T.L. Moffat IV

*Gordon Moffat with his DP, accompanied by his wife, Olive, and their children, Robert and Flora. Two friends look on.*
– Courtesy Bob Moffat

*First boat? The old family washtub was an ideal boat for young children, like Flora Moffat, seen here in 1929.*

In the early thirties boats became more streamlined and sporty. The planing hull replaced the old displacement hulls. The configuration of the cockpit changed, with the motor mounted behind the driver. Earl Barnes of Bracebridge pioneered these streamlined hulls. In 1936 he designed two torpedo-shaped boats. One built by Minett-Shields was shown at the New York boat show. The other was shown at the Toronto boat show and was purchased by Howard Charlton.

In the late 1930s Duke came out with its Playmate designs. These were perfect for Penlake. A number of outboards also began to appear, generally on small skiffs. The larger and heavier hulls required a much larger motor, and as outboard engines were not reliable and had to be pull-started, they were not too popular.

Then came the 1950s. Outboard motors were not only relatively light, but powerful, reliable, and electric-started. With their light cedar-strip hulls they could accommodate a family and pull a waterskier. These cheap, manoeuvrable, and functional boats graced most Muskoka Lakes.

Now, in the 1990s, boats are brought in by trailer from far and near, resulting in a significant increase not only in the number of boats but also pollution. To the chagrin of cottagers who remember simpler, quieter times, many of today's boats are too large, too noisy, and too fast.

*RDM*

*First boat. Flora and Bob Moffat in 1929*

*Thomas Lang Moffat III with Don Moffat in a Sponson canoe. Note the "Sponson," or air chambers, which are built into the gunwale for added flotation.*
– Photos courtesy Bob Moffat

94

## Kanuck

Jointly owned from 1912 to 1920 by the three Moffat brothers, T.L., F.W. and J.K., who had adjoining cottages on Springsyde, the *Kanuck* was a 26-foot launch powered by a two-cylinder Buffalo engine. It was capable of speeds of 10 to 12 mph, and was used for trips to Huntsville and family outings.

## G.E. Henderson's

White and narrow, about 30 feet long, this launch was already old in the 1920s, so it probably dated to about 1915. Powered by a huge six-cylinder Sterling engine, the Henderson boat was fast and offered an impressive ride.

## A.B. Moffat Boat

Built by Gidley Boat Company in Penetanguishene in about 1915, this 26-foot runabout was owned by A.B. Moffat — one of the five Moffat brothers on the lake after the turn of the century. Although quite fast for its time, the boat tended to roll in rough water.

*This 1913 photo of the* Kanuck *shows, left to right: Eileen Moffat, Dorothy Moffat, Ella Moffat holding Jack, Bea Moffat, ?, James Moffat, Agnes Moffat, F.W. Moffat, Dr. McPhedran, ?, Don Moffat, Lang Moffat, and Freddy Moffat.*
– Courtesy the Moffat family

## Purdy-Mansell Boat

In 1922 this beautiful light mahogany launch, a classic Ditchburn, was delivered new to its joint purchasers at Springsyde. With a huge cockpit fitted with movable wicker chairs, it was powered by a four-cylinder Kermath engine capable of speeds up to 17 mph.

## Black Shadow

So called for its black paint, this speedboat was owned by C.O. Shaw, owner of the tannery, the Navigation Company, and Bigwin Inn. It was frequently seen tearing across Penlake on the way to North Portage, where it got hauled up onto the flat car and taken to South Portage by the Little Train. There it was launched for the ride to Bigwin. Powered by a huge six-cylinder Sterling engine, it was capable of speeds up to 35 mph.

*Earl Barnes built the Billie-Bea I for the Charlton family, who used the 24-foot mahogany runabout from 1932 to 1936. A Barnes trademark, an Indian head, was mounted on the bow.*
– Courtesy the Charlton family

96

### *Billie  Bea  I  ~  1932 - 1936*

Dr. and Mrs. Howard Charlton owned this 24-foot mahogany runabout, with its handsome fittings and deck. Built in Bracebridge by Earl Barnes and delivered new in the summer of 1932, it was powered by a six-cylinder Chrysler engine.

### *Billie  Bea  II  ~  1936 - 1975*

Earl Barnes built the Charltons' second boat, a 26-footer, using an advanced design for the hull. It was delivered new in the summer of 1936 and was originally powered by a straight-eight Chrysler 125 hp engine, making it capable of speeds of 35 mph.

*Bea Charlton and young Bill in the cockpit of the* Billie-Bea II, *one of the two boats that Earl Barnes designed with a "torpedo" stern.*
– Courtesy the Charlton family

## Evangeline

Everett Barker of North Portage owned the *Evangeline,* a beautiful 28-foot mahogany craft built by Ditchburn in Gravenhurst sometime before 1920. Barker was known for using the boat's speed of 25 mph to come out and circle the *Algonquin* just before it docked. The captain of the *Algonquin* took exception to Barker's antics, often shaking his fist at him and blowing the horn.

**The** Evangeline, *owned by Everett Barker.*
– Courtesy Don Marshall

### The Betty Lou

Capable of reaching speeds of 28 mph, the *Betty Lou* was built by Earl Barnes of Bracebridge for the Musselman family. The 26-foot mahogany runabout was powered by a six-cylinder Chrysler engine and delivered new in 1935.

### Will-o-the-Wisp

Owned by Lang Moffat III, this 18-foot sport boat was built by Earl Barnes of Bracebridge. It was one of twin boats, identical in design and specification; the other was owned by Jim Moffat. Both boats were delivered in the summer of 1934. Lang raced the *Will-o-the-Wisp* at the CNE and won in both 1936 and 1937. Powered by a Chrysler Ace six-cylinder, 100 hp engine, it attained speeds as great as 38 mph.

### Slo-Poke ~ 1936

One of the first high-powered hydroplanes on Penlake, the *Slo-Poke* was the proud possession of Don Moffat in the mid-1930s. With a length of 14 feet, it won the "free for all" boat race in the 1936 Penlake regatta.

*RDM,*
*from notes of the Reverend Jack Moffat*

*The* Betty Lou
– Courtesy Claude Musselman

*Above: Art Blackburn driving the Drew-Brook launch with Mollie Drew-Brook at his side as they pass below the drawbridge in Huntsville. This is a good view of this streamlined Earl Barnes boat in the early 1930s.*
– Courtesy Mollie Drew-Brook Roden

*Above right: Ralph Dilworth at the wheel of the Dilworth launch.*
– Courtesy Sylvia Dilworth Hurst-Brown

*Middle: Dot Allport sitting in an early outboard built by Century and named the* **Century Traveler**.
– Courtesy Jack Moffat

*Bottom: The* **Nancy**, *driven by James Moffat, circa 1937. Built by Earl Barnes, this boat was a twin to the* **Will-o-the-Wisp**.
– Courtesy Nancy Moffat Scarth

# MOTORBOAT RACES

No ONE KNOWS EXACTLY when boat races became part of the regatta, but by the mid-1930s the event had generated considerable interest.

Many early races followed a course defined by the buoy marking the shoal near Springsyde and a second buoy in Put-in-Bay. During the era of grand motor launches, it was fascinating to see Ditchburn boats competing with ones built by Greavette and Barnes. Earl Barnes's boats were invariably the winners — until Don Moffat arrived with *Slo-Poke,* his new 34-horsepower hydroplane, which ran circles around everyone else.

Lang Moffat's *Will-o-the-Wisp*, designed by Barnes, won first in its class at the CNE boat races in 1936 and 1937. The 1937 win was because the *Will-o-the-Wisp* was the only boat capable of completing the course in the stormy waters off the Exhibition waterfront!

Boat races moved from North Portage to Deerhurst in the mid-1950s. Young Bill Waterhouse, a racing enthusiast and keen competitor, set a course off Deerhurst wharf. Each summer this traditional counter-clockwise course with a twist — that is, a right-hand turn out from the dock — provided some anxious and spectacular moments for competitors and spectators alike. Bill's ability to keep his super-light boat upright while powered by an overweight motor almost always made him the winner.

Classes were set according to engine horsepower; there were the open outboard and open inboard races. Between races, competitors furiously hoisted higher horsepower motors on light and sometimes flimsy craft, driven with reckless abandon by the likes of John and Dick Moffat, Bob Broad, John Stuart, Tom Todd, and Joel Kimmel.

Somewhat more sophisticated equipment appeared in the late 1950s. Outside competitors appeared, including the Orville Wright family with their Mercury-powered Aristo Crafts.

Some competitors seriously developed that extra competitive edge. Mike Weaber, for instance, used to take his boat out of the water a week before race day, drying it out to decrease its weight.

During the early 1950s Doug Moffat competed in sanctioned inboard hydro-plane races in the 48-cubic-inch class with *Little Miss Moffat* and the 135-cubic-inch class with *School Days*. In the late 1950s and early 1960s Norm Moffat won races in Muskoka with his 50-horsepower Aristo Craft and 100-horsepower Switzer Craft.

As motors increased in size and sophistication, it was impossible to program races of equal class. Safety also became an issue. Accordingly, in 1963 motorboat races were eliminated from the regatta.

*RDM, with Norm Moffat*

*Powered by an early Johnson motor, the* Baby Hornet *was often called "the speediest boat on the lake." In the boat are Norman Moffat and Margaret Griffis (soon-to-be Mrs. Moffat), in 1940.*
– Courtesy Mrs. Norman Moffat

*The art of rowing was learned at an early age.*
*Don Moffat, circa 1910.*
– Courtesy T.L. Moffat

# ROWING

EARLY ROWBOATS, OR SKIFFS, plied the lake during cottage construction, carrying supplies. These craft, pointed at each end, had more beam than canoes and, with two bench seats in the middle, significantly more carrying capacity. Equipped with double oars, they were capable of significant speed and quite stable in rough water — ideal, then, for a family of four or for transporting provisions from the North Portage store.

These boats were especially popular through the 1930s and 1940s. Today many have been restored and make their annual appearance in the regatta, heeding the starter's command: "Are you ready? Row!"

Competitive rowing, or sculling, was brought to the lake in the 1930s by Jack and Norm Moffat. In 1935 Norman began to train in earnest, using a training shell, for the North American schoolboy sculling championship in Philadelphia. Penlake, with its tranquil early-morning waters, was ideal for sculling. In Philadelphia, he placed second, but the following year he won the inter-scholastic sculling championship in Worcester, Massachusetts. Dick Stockwell, the trainer of the Toronto Argonauts, was hired to instil some training discipline in Norman that year.

The highlight of Norman's rowing career was his participation in the single scull at England's prestigious Royal Henley Regatta in 1936. He lost this race to the great Joe Burke. Norman, Jr., continued this rowing tradition by training at the lake and competing in numerous sculling events, as well as taking the stroke position for the University of Western Ontario Varsity Eight.

Carol Eastmure was attracted to this graceful sport, and after sitting in Norman's racing scull, she became hooked on it. She recognizes that the Penlake regatta was influential in fostering her strong competitive spirit. Having rowed for the McMaster University team, she successfully gained a seat as stroke for the National Women's Eight in time for the 1976 Montreal Olympics — the first year that female rowers were represented at the games. In the final race, the Canadian boat came within half a deck of placing third. Carol and her team went on to win a bronze medal at the World Championships in Amsterdam in 1977. Rowing continued to dominate her life; she became a national development coach and married former Olympic rower, Brian Love.

*Norm Moffat, Jr.*

*Norm Moffat and Norm Jr. in their sculls.*
– Courtesy Mrs. Norman Moffat

*Carol Eastmure (Love), stroke, Canadian National Women's Eight, 1976 Olympics.*
– Courtesy Dorothy Mansell Eastmure

# SAILING

Early attempts at sailing on Penlake ranged from hoisting a big sheet on a rough-hewn wooden raft to raising a triangular sail on a canoe with leeboards fastened near the bow seat. Canoes were usually fitted with a rudder, but steering was often done by the skilful use of the helmsman's paddle.

These homemade sailboats eventually gave way to professionally built boats, such as Lakefields and Akroyds. Sailing was then included in the regatta.

Usually the sailboat design decided the winner, but on one occasion the craftiness of the sailor seemed to pay off. Lang Moffat, Sr., entered the sailing race in his little 12-foot pram, and not unexpectedly, he was dead last from the start. Then to everyone's surprise, he seemed to pick up wind from nowhere. He caught up and passed the others, winning by a comfortable margin.

After the race, a crowd gathered to admire this phenomenal little craft. With a sly grin, Lang moved the tarpaulin on the bottom of the boat. Everyone laughed at the sight of the small outboard motor on the bottom of the boat.

For years the Penlake sailors talked about how great it would be if everyone bought the same class of sailboat so that races would be determined by the sailor's skill, not by the boat design. Dr. Gordon Moffat was a leading advocate of this idea. In the early 1960s Gordon's son, Bob, bought an Albacore. Coincidentally, the man renting at the Drewbrook cottage also owned an Albacore.

For two years they raced their Albacores around the lake with obvious enjoyment. When, not wanting to miss out on the fun, Russell Eastmure and Ralph Thompson both bought Albacores, the Penlake Yacht Club was born.

Dr. Gordon Moffat's children — Flora, Carol, and Bob — donated a trophy in their father's memory to be awarded to the annual champion of the weekly Albacore races. The club was now well on its way. Bill and Kae McCann donated the Master's Trophy to recognize the oldtimers in the sailing races.

The club grew until it was not uncommon to see a fleet of ten to fifteen Albacores racing each weekend. When the Penlake Invitational was held, boats from Lake of Bays, Mary Lake, and Fairy Lake would compete after a lunchtime barbecue and pre-race skippers' meeting. It was thrilling to see more than twenty boats jockeying for position at the starting line.

The regatta sailing race was an open-class event, but it excluded the Albacores. Wilf Houghton, whose love of sailing continued from his association with the Royal Canadian Navy, donated the Houghton Trophy for the regatta race, hoping to encourage sailors of all ages.

Alas, like so many other things on Penlake, sailing has come full circle. The weekly Albacore races, as well as the annual regatta races, today have only two or three participants.

*RDM*

*Sailing in 1918. Left to right: Elizabeth Brinkman, Helen Brown (Cook),*
L.D. Brown Jr. *at the tiller, Margaret (Spurr), and Crawf Brown.*

– Courtesy the Spurr family

*Two Albacores: Ralph and Betty Jane Thompson in 2424, and Rosemary Eastmure-Charron and John Eastmure in 3062.*
– Courtesy Dorothy Mansell Eastmure

# WATERSKIING

CLARK HILL, who married Aileen Moffat, was a water-sport enthusiast. In the late 1930s he erected a fifteen-foot slide and a three-metre diving board on Springsyde wharf. His real forte was aquaplaning behind his Horace Dodge inboard, a noisy boat with very little freeboard. It was ideally suited to aquaplaning, but not for rough water!

Under Clark's tutelage, his children, Moffat and Marly, as well as his nephew Vic Stewart, became expert aquaplaners. They often rode side by side and standing on chairs.

By 1939 the Hill family was searching for alternatives to aquaplaning. Rumor had it that people were starting to plane on skis, so the Hills decided to give it a try. Not really knowing how it was done, their first attempts were with a pair of ultra-light cedar skis eight feet long and eight inches wide, fitted with a sort of harness and pulled in the same fashion as an aquaplane. By the end of the summer the skiers tried hanging on to the rope themselves, controlling the skis by their feet and distribution of weight. In short order, Moffat, Marly, and Vic became expert skiers. Moffat went on to compete at the Canadian National Exhibition, and Marley joined its waterskiing troupe. She later became one of the first Canadians to perform at Cypress Gardens in Florida.

These water activities gained in popularity and inventiveness. The Dilworths used a wide plank platform, not unlike a kitchen door, which they often lent to the Spurrs. The Spurr boat would pull the board topped with a pyramid — the Eastmures' black Labrador, Sam, straddled by Ian Eastmure with Gish Foster on his shoulders. Bob Newton of Put-in-Bay became expert on a disc, not only doing 360s, but riding the disc perched on a ladder!

Near Deerhurst, Bob Broad and his friends worked on trick and competitive skiing. In 1949 his family acquired a pair of secondhand waterskis from a man in Oshawa. The seven-foot cedar skis were about eight inches wide, with grooves on the bottom like snow skis, and no keels. Bob taught a lot of people to ski in the early 1950s. He entered the Ontario Championships as a junior and skied in competitions in Orillia and Owen Sound. In 1953 he was runner-up to the Canadian champion in the Men's Open waterskiing championships at the CNE. In 1953 Clark and Moffat Hill became actively involved in the Canadian Waterskiing Association.

For a few years waterskiing was a regatta event. Like motorboat races, it was held the week before the main regatta. A slalom course was set up along the golf-course shore by the number-two fairway. This provided a straight run, as well as an excellent vantage point for spectators. Since the event took much time and effort to organize, it is not surprising that it did not last long.

*RDM*

*Surfboarding: Beverley Darling, the Foster boathouse in the background.*
– Courtesy Anna Mirrette Darling

*Waterski jumping: Bob Broad. Bob Broad built the first waterski jump on Penlake*
*around 1950. Pow Wow Point is in the background.*
– Courtesy Bob Broad

*Waterskier Cathy Moffat*
– Courtesy Bob Moffat

*Regatta*
*Memories*

*Top: Paddling for a win!*
*Kate (Holloway) Fusco and Whitney Holloway.*
*Above: The War Canoe in the mid-1980s*
– Photos courtesy Whitney Holloway
*Right: The Junior regatta at Springsyde*
– Courtesy Dorothy Mansell Eastmure

# PENLAKE REGATTA

THE EARLIEST RECORD OF A REGATTA on Penlake is in the Friday, August 24, 1900, edition of the *Huntsville Forester*.

On August 25, 1901, the *Forester* chronicled Penlake's second regatta, held on August 14. Mayor Hart of Huntsville declared the day a "civic holiday enabling residents of Huntsville to attend the event in large numbers." Competitors paid an entrance fee of ten and fifteen cents, down from the twenty-five-cent fee charged the previous year.

Early records of Penlake regattas are sketchy. The first two were well documented, but few records remain of subsequent events until after the Second World War.

Oral histories validate their existence. Helen Brown Cook, who first came to Penlake in 1908, recalls: "There were events of considerable proportion at Deerhurst and later, the event moved around. One year it might be held in Grassmere, another at Winoka. There weren't any held during the war."

Regattas were numbered before and after the Second World War, but the chronology is confusing. Regattas held at Springsyde can be traced as far back as 1914. At some unknown period a second series of numbers was introduced. This system prevented an accurate tally of the actual number of regattas held. In 1991 the phrase "A Tradition Since 1900" was added to the annual program and the specific number was eliminated.

The first regatta had eleven events. Today there are nineteen morning events for the junior program and thirty-one afternoon events in the senior program. Canoeing, sculling, swimming, and diving contests predominate, and in the morning foot races and other children's events are held. The afternoon is rounded out with tilting and a canoe tug-of-war, along with a ladies' nail-driving contest.

The "slippery pole" used to be a perennial favourite. A liberally greased horizontal pole had to be traversed by a contestant. Inopportune falls and injuries were not uncommon, which likely led to the disappearance of this contest.

One of the most popular events is the war-canoe race. Strictly speaking, a war canoe has only four paddlers, but in practice no entry is disqualified. While a canoe with an army of paddlers might appear to have an advantage, the winning canoe is always manned by four young men. One year the cocky crew of the *Wolf Bay Boat*, buoyed by a decisive win, engraved their trophy for that year's win and the next year's as well! But when next year came, the *Wolf Bay Boat* succeeded in winning only narrowly. The team prudently elected never to second-guess chance again.

For many years the women's committee of the Peninsula Lake Associa-

## THE HUNTSVILLE LAKE ASSOCIATION HOLDS THE FIRST IN A SERIES OF REGATTAS AT DEERHURST

### *MOST SUCCESSFULLY ARRANGED AND CARRIED OUT*

The Huntsville Lakes Association may well feel proud of their first regatta held at Deerhurst on Friday last, August 17. The whole matter was hurriedly arrranged, advertising matter was out only two days previous, but these drawbacks seemed to have little if any effect on the success of the event.

The steamer *Empress*, with 150 people on board including the Association officers, left Town Dock at 1:15 and upon its arrival found that the head committee at Deerhurst had made every arrangement necessary so that very little delay was experienced in getting the different events underway.

At 2:15, Judges Messers Mathews and Batehart took their positions at the finishing post. Starter H.S. May swung into line and Secretary/Treasurer J.E. Fisher called the first event and the day's sport was on. From start to finish, no disputes were heard, no dissatisfaction expressed at the judges' decisions and no disappointment was felt by those who lined the sloping shore. It was an afternoon of real enjoyment and the committee in charge, together with those who took part in the different events, are highly congratulated upon the completion of the arrangements and ultimate success of the regatta.

| MENS SINGLE SCULL | | MENS SINGLE CANOE | |
|---|---|---|---|
| 1st | Hollingshead | 1st | J. Remeys |
| 2nd | Brabant | 2nd | O.D. Tait |

| LADIES SINGLE SCULL | | GUNWALE RACE | |
|---|---|---|---|
| 1st | Miss Irene May | 1st | S. Hollingshead |
| 2nd | Mrs. McCullough | 2nd | E.S. Anderson |

| MENS DOUBLE SCULL | | CRAB RACE | |
|---|---|---|---|
| 1st | Hollingshead Brothers | 1st | Hollingshead |
| 2nd | McCullough and Anderson | 2nd | J. Lightbody |

| MENS SWIMMING RACE | | MENS DOUBLE CANOE | |
|---|---|---|---|
| 1st | Jamie Lightbody | 1st | Remey Brothers |
| 2nd | W. Delafosse | 2nd | Anderson and Fowler |

| BOYS SWIMMING RACE | | LADIES & GENTS TANDEM | |
|---|---|---|---|
| 1st | M. Thompson | 1st | Miss A. Yellowlees and Mr. Delafosse |
| 2nd | D. Kinton | 2nd | Miss M. Yellowlees and Mr. Jeffrey |

| LADIES SINGLE CANOE | |
|---|---|
| 1st | Miss M. Yellowlees |
| 2nd | Miss Middleton |

*The article about the first regatta on Penlake from the* Huntsville Forester, *August 24, 1900.*

tion organized the regatta. Eventually, however, the victors of one year's event became the convenors of the next.

Also, for many years, cottagers donated money for prizes and trophies. Teenagers were assigned to certain shores, and they walked from cottage to cottage, receipt book in hand, to meet the budget. In those days ten dollars purchased a silver cup, which the recipient could keep — donors often received a thank-you note. There were felt crests for winners, as well as for runners-up. A second-place finish won the participant a bottle of perfume, a new tackle box, or a life jacket. But inflation and permanent trophies have changed all that. Today prizes are given only for the foot races and nail-driving contest.

At one time, competitors who won a trophy for three consecutive years could claim it as their own. This led to the disappearance of a number of historic trophies from the annual competition. At least one trophy has been found on another lake and brought home.

Over the years the regatta has been a constant, and the trophies and their inscriptions represent a facet of Penlake history. As generations change, regatta attendance fluctuates, but at the 1992 regatta there were so many contenders in the junior program that some of the events had to be run in heats. The future of the Penlake regatta promises to be bright.

*ISA*

*"On your mark, get set..."*
*Men's swimming race.*
*Left to right: ?, Graeme Eastmure, ?,*
*Brian Love, Norm Moffat,*
*John Eastmure, Trip Sieber, ?,*
*and Storm Purdy.*
– Courtesy Whitney Holloway

# TILTING WITH THE BIG BOYS

IN OUR YOUNGER DAYS my partner and I welcomed all comers to the art of tilting — until, that is, the regatta in which we faced Whipper Billy Watson and his partner, who were summering at Cedar Grove. Not wanting to provoke the famous wrestler by throwing the first blow, we tactfully retreated. In an attempt to press an attack, the Whipper and his partner drove forward. With their combined weights allowing them only half an inch of freeboard, along with the slight unbalancing of the canoe, they promptly swamped. My partner and I, in most modest fashion, humbly accepted this victory, for who else had ever defeated the great Whipper without even landing a single blow!

*RDM*

*Tilting with the big boys.*
– Courtesy Whitney Holloway

## CHAMPIONSHIP TROPHIES

*A complete listing of all who have become "champions" since the regatta began is not available. However, the four major trophies, with inscriptions dating back to 1941, read like a history of the lake. The five trophies whose inscriptions are listed on the following pages remind us of the many families and generations who have been a part of Penlake.*

FOUR TROPHIES honour the overall male and female winners of the Junior and Senior events of the regatta:

### EASTMURE TROPHY

This stately championship trophy is inscribed "The North Muskoka Lakes Association for Annual Competition, by A.W. Eastmure, 1941."

Wyburn Eastmure, a regatta starter for many years, enjoyed competitive paddling in Toronto. Nearly all his descendants on Penlake are skilled canoeists and have excelled in most regatta events. The first recipient of this historic award was Ian Eastmure, Wyburn's son. The trophy bears witness that no regattas were held during the years of the Second World War, from 1942 to 1945. Before there was a separate women's trophy, several women won this hotly contested award.

### SISSONS TROPHY

Awarded to the Women's Senior Champion, this trophy was first presented in 1964 to recognize the many fine female contenders in regatta events. Charles and Joan Sissons gave this trophy in honour of their four daughters: Sherry, Carol, Judy, and Kathy. Joan Sissons ably served for a number of years as president of the Peninsula Lake Association.

### WAWANEIKA TROPHY

Dean Ross recalls that *wawaneika* means "little western breezes." A number of families, including Dr. Ross's, have owned the Wawaneika cottage, which the Barker family built in the early 1900s.

Later the Nowes and the Thurmans enjoyed summers at Wawaneika. They jointly donated the trophy in 1954 to honour the Boys' Champion. Until 1964 girls also competed for this prize.

### HENDERSON TROPHY

The Henderson family first presented this award in 1964 to the Girls' (fifteen and under) Champion. Prior to this, girls competed with boys for the Junior Championship, winning five out of ten such competitions.

| LADIES' SENIOR CHAMPIONSHIP SISSONS TROPHY | |
|---|---|
| 1964 | Susan Moffat |
| 1965 | Dorothy Hodgins |
| 1966 | Carol Sissons |
| 1967 | Susan Moffat |
| 1968 | Dorothy Fraser |
| 1969 | Jamee Todd |
| 1970 | Kathy Sissons & Sheila Houghton |
| 1971 | Judith Sissons |
| 1972 | (name missing) |
| 1973 | Carol Eastmure |
| 1974 | Carol Eastmure |
| 1975 | Debbie Eastmure |
| 1976 | (name missing) |
| 1977 | Debbie Eastmure & Margo Hudson |
| 1978 | Debbie Eastmure |
| 1979 | Carol Eastmure |
| 1980 | Jayne Woodcock |
| 1981 | Jayne Woodcock |
| 1982 | Debbie Eastmure |
| 1983 | Debbie Eastmure |
| 1984 | Debbie Court |
| 1985 | Whitney Holloway |
| 1986 | Whitney Holloway |
| 1987 | Jamee Todd |
| 1988 | Carol Love |
| 1989 | Carol Love |
| 1990 | Debbie Court |
| 1991 | Carol Love |
| 1992 | Carol Love & Debbie Court |

# EVENT TROPHIES

A number of trophies have been donated over the years to honour the winner of particular regatta events:

## APPLETON TROPHY

It began as a joke. After winning the nail-driving event for a number of years, Dibbie Spurr Appleton took a large dock spike and hammered it partway into a beam block. (Both were remnants from ice damage to the dock.) The resulting "trophy" was brought to its first regatta dance in a plain brown wrapper. While of no monetary value, the trophy gained in historic value when, in 1991, the old paper winners' labels were replaced with permanent brass plaques. Women who own up to being over twenty-five compete for the Appleton Trophy.

## BLAKE–WALTON TROPHY

Perhaps the most unusual of all the trophies, this former silver sugar bowl was reborn as the prize for the Ladies' Single Scull. Evelyn Walton Kimmel Taylor, whose family once owned the Portage Store, presented it in 1987.

## BRENCIAGLIA TROPHY

In 1987 Susan (Moffat) and John Brenciaglia first presented this trophy to the winner of the Girls' Single Canoe. Chrissy Brenciaglia, Susan and John's daughter, won it that year on her way to taking the Girls' Junior Championship. Susan, a fourth-generation Penlaker and once a Junior Champion herself, continues to be a contender in the regatta.

## BURROW TROPHY

Attorney Garth Burrow and his wife, Ginny, first presented the trophy in 1991 to the winner of the Boys' Swim event. The Burrow family settled on the Pow Wow shore in the 1950s.

## CHARLTON TROPHY

The Charlton Trophy is one of the older awards. Dr. and Mrs. Howard Charlton donated it to honour the victor of the Boys' Single Canoe race.

## D. EASTMURE COURT TROPHY

First presented in 1991, this trophy is for the Girls' Swim event. The donor, Deborah Court, has competed in national meets. A frequent winner of the Sissons Trophy, she has won the Women's Swim event at least ten times.

## DR. F.D. CRUICKSHANK MEMORIAL TROPHY

Dr. Fred, as he was affectionately known, lived in a Springsyde cottage. Former President of the Penlake Association, Dr. Fred was often sought during medical emergencies. His children also took up medicine.

| SENIOR CHAMPIONSHIP EASTMURE TROPHY WINNERS | |
| --- | --- |
| 1941 | Ian Eastmure |
| 1946 | T. Lang Moffat & Ian Eastmure |
| 1947 | Ian Eastmure |
| 1948 | Donald Eastmure |
| 1949 | Donald Eastmure & Ian Eastmure |
| 1950 | Ian Eastmure & James D. Moffat |
| 1951 | Bob McMillin & James Green |
| 1952 | James Moffat, Jane Cruickshank & James McMillin |
| 1953 | Alec MacLellan |
| 1954 | Cathy Reid |
| 1955 | Cathy Reid |
| 1956 | Cathy Reid |
| 1957 | Cathy Reid |
| 1958 | Jamee Wadsworth |
| 1959 | John McIntosh |
| 1960 | Cathy Reid |
| 1961 | Peter Moffat |
| 1962 | Norman Moffat |
| 1963 | Jamee Wadsworth |
| 1964 | Norman Moffat |
| 1965 | Norman Moffat |
| 1966 | Joel Kimmel |
| 1967 | Norman Moffat |
| 1968 | Norman Moffat |
| 1969 | Peter Heenan |
| 1970 | Norman Moffat |
| 1971 | Norman Moffat |
| 1972 | Norman Moffat |
| 1973 | Norman Moffat |
| 1974 | Peter Moffat |
| 1975 | Norman Moffat |
| 1976 | John Eastmure |
| 1977 | John Eastmure |
| 1978 | John Eastmure |
| 1979 | John Eastmure |
| 1980 | John Eastmure & T.L. Moffat |
| 1981 | John Eastmure |
| 1982 | David Hughes |
| 1983 | Norman Moffat |
| 1984 | Gordon Moffat |
| 1985 | John Eastmure |
| 1986 | John Eastmure |
| 1987 | John Eastmure |
| 1988 | Dick Eastmure |
| 1989 | John Eastmure |
| 1990 | John Eastmure |
| 1991 | John Eastmure |
| 1992 | John Eastmure |

# Regatta
# Trophies

*Purdy and Mansell trophies*

*A champion's haul*

*Awards collection in the Eastmure cottage*
– Photos by Dibbie Spurr Appleton

Many regatta events begin or end at the Cruickshank family dock. This award, given by his descendants in memory of one of the lake's longtime residents, is presented to the winner of the Men's Double Canoe race.

## HALL TROPHY

Monteith E. Hall had a lumber business in Kitchener and came to Penlake in 1908. His son, Monteith C. Hall, took over the cottage in 1924 and remained on the lake until the property was sold to Olive Musselman in 1930.

The Hall Trophy is the oldest still in circulation. It was first presented to the winner of the Mens' Single Canoe in 1925. Gaps in the chronology of winners attest to the fact that the Hall Trophy has disappeared from the lake on at least one occasion, no doubt won by a visitor to Penlake. Spotted on a mantel far from Penlake shores, the trophy was returned.

## JOHN J. HAY MEMORIAL TROPHY

A physician from Pittsburgh, Pennsylvania, Dr. John Hay came to Penlake in the 1940s. Almost a scratch golfer, he took charge of the junior golf tournaments for many years. The Hay cottage was located just off the old seventh tee of the golf course — a convenient place for a family with three other good golfers, Trudy (Spurr) Hay and their sons, David and John, Jr. The Hay Trophy for Mixed Double Canoe (fifteen and under) was presented to the association in 1987 in memory of their father by David and John, who live in Scottsdale, Arizona.

## HODGINS TROPHY

Donated by the Hodgins family of Isle Dunelg, this trophy recognizes promising young divers. The presentation of this lovely silver cup depends upon the condition of the Springsyde dock, for when ice damage has been severe, the diving board can be often close to or even under the water! Dodie (Hodgins) Nilsson often serves as judge of both the Senior and Junior diving events, assisted by John Stuart.

## J. D. HUDSON TROPHY

A judge in Ontario's York County Court, Drew Hudson was introduced to the lake by Russell Eastmure. He raised his five children in their Springsyde cottage. All were avid regatta contenders who were often led to victory by the senior Hudson.

First presented in the 1970s, the silver cup is mounted on a base to which a second base has been attached to accommodate the names of winners. The Mixed Double Canoe race, for which the Hudson trophy is awarded, is a highlight of the regatta.

*The oldest trophy still in circulation for the Penlake Regatta is the Hall Trophy, first presented in 1925.*

### MENS' SINGLE CANOE HALL TROPHY

| | |
|---|---|
| 1925 | Jack Moffat |
| 1932-36 | Lorne Wright |
| 1937-39 | Lorne Wright |
| 1940-41 | Ian Eastmure |
| 1946 | Don Cruickshank |
| 1952 | Bob McMillin |
| 1953 | (winning name missing) |
| 1954 | Jim Moffat |
| 1959 | Phil MacDonald |
| 1960-61 | Paul Moffat |
| 1962 | Bob McMillin |
| 1963 | Norm Moffat |
| 1964-68 | Bob McMillin |
| 1969 | Peter Heenan |
| 1970 | Norm Moffat |
| 1971 | Norm Moffat |
| 1972 | Drew Hudson |
| 1973-75 | Norm Moffat |
| 1976 | John Eastmure |
| 1977-79 | Ross Hudson |
| 1980 | Norm Moffat |
| 1981 | Andrew McMillin |
| 1982 | David Hughes |
| 1983-86 | Norm Moffat |
| 1987 | Ross Hudson |
| 1988 | Norm Moffat |
| 1989 | John Eastmure |
| 1990-91 | Bruce Rudolph |
| 1992 | John Eastmure |

*At one time the Hall Trophy disappeared from Penlake, but was later found in a cottage on Lake Muskoka and returned to Penlake. It is assumed that a guest won the trophy and took it home as a souvenir.*

## PROGRAMME
### OF EVENTS

+ +

— FIFTEENTH —
Pen Lake Annual Regatta
AT POW WOW POINT
August 4th, 1934

FIRST EVENT STARTS AT 2 O'CLOCK E.D.S. TIME

## THE LOVE CUP

This charming silver trophy, awarded to the winner of the Girl's Single Scull, is aptly named. It was first presented in 1991 by Carol (Eastmure) and Brian Love, who met and fell in love while competing for Canada in the 1976 Olympics. Carol served as stroke for the Women's Eight; Brian competed in the Men's Pair.

## LUCAS–MARSHALL MEMORIAL TROPHY

For many years, Frederick Lucas of Toronto, comptroller for the Purdy-Mansell Corporation, served as starter at the regatta, using a megaphone. His only daughter, Audrey, married Edward Marshall, and Allan, their son, presented this trophy for the Men's Single Scull in 1987. The larger trophy came with twenty smaller cups, which may be kept by the winner of the permanent trophy.

## W. F. MacLennan Memorial Trophy

The War Canoe race traditionally clears the beach of all available canoes. The MacLennan family's association with the Springsyde shore dates back to the 1930s. W. Fraser MacLennan served for twenty years as the regatta recorder, succeeding Fred Woods. The War Canoe was the favourite event of his youth. The trophy was first presented in 1967.

## MANSELL TROPHY

Evelyn (Mansell) Zering of Toronto first presented this trophy to Ben Spurr and Sandy Holloway for Tilting in 1957. It bears the name of her father, George Richard Mansell, whose descendants compete in today's regattas.

The trophy is a fine example of recycling. It was originally presented at the Toronto Flower Show, where it honoured the prize-winning dahlias of William Mansell, George Richard's father.

## McCREADY TROPHY

This trophy was first presented for the Gunwale Race in the 1987 regatta by Bill and Marge McCready of Pittsburgh, Pennsylvania. The race requires participants to paddle a short course with both feet braced on the gunwales of a canoe. The field of entrants is small and predominantly male, and competition is extremely keen.

Bill's father, Dr. James McCready, was an early cottager on the lake and the owner of the golf club. The generosity of the McCready family in making the facilities of the golf club available over the years is legendary.

## DON AND ISABEL McINTOSH TROPHY

Presented for the Girls' Double Scull, this award was originally given in 1987. Don McIntosh, a Toronto lawyer, was lured to Penlake by the Eastmures, staying first at Deerhurst before purchasing the old Johnstone cottage. As well as gaining a reputation as a fine golfer, Don also served for many years on the Peninsula Lake Association board of directors, where his keen wit was much appreciated.

# McKeon Trophy

When Dan and Ann McKeon gave the winner of the Girls' Double Canoe race this new trophy in 1987, they were the new kids on the block, having purchased the Kirkpatrick cottage near Tally Ho in 1979. Lured to the area for skiing, the family owned a chalet at Hidden Valley. When Dan retired from his corrugated-box business in Toronto, he and Ann chose to consolidate vacations; they sold both the chalet and their cottage at Lake Simcoe and became Penlake cottagers.

# D.R. Moffat Trophy

A gift of Donald R. Moffat, this trophy is presented to the winning team of four persons in the Canoe Tug-a-War. In this event, two canoes are linked by a length of rope, and the teams, paddling in opposite directions, must drag their opponents across a marker to win. The match is fought ferociously and often results in at least one boat's capsizing.

The third youngest of six children, Don Moffat was a longtime Penlake resident before moving to Lake of Bays. His sons, Paul and Michael, were active regatta participants. The D.R. Moffat cottage is now owned by Joan Sissons-Beatty.

# John King Moffat, Jr., Memorial Cup

The eldest son of the Rev. John King Moffat, whose family cottage is near the old portage, J.K. Moffat, Jr., was tragically killed, with his wife, Marlene, in a freak automobile accident while on a pilgrimage in Turkey. The trophy was given in 1988 by his sons John, David, and Steven, and by his brothers, Dick and Peter. Awarded for the Boys' Double Scull, to date it has always been won by a Moffat.

# Lang Moffat Trophy

This is an older trophy, although it has not been in recent circulation for long. It was reintroduced in 1987, after the death of Lang Moffat III, on the fiftieth anniversary of its first presentation in 1937 for the Boys' (nine and under) Double Scull. Doug and Lang Moffat were the first winners. While this race is no longer on the regatta program, the original inscription has not been removed. A later inscription, for the Mens' Double Scull, has been added.

# Norman Moffat Challenge Trophy

Presented to the winner of the Boys' Single Scull, this unique trophy, a silver tray, was given in memory of Norman Moffat by his wife, Margaret, and their children, Susan (Brenciaglia), Norman, and Ann.

The youngest of T.L. Moffat II's six children, Norman was an avid rower and regatta contender. He was so popular that his photo even appeared on the cover of two regatta programs. His children and grandchildren have continued to excel in competitive events, particularly rowing.

| BOYS' CHAMPIONSHIP 15 & UNDER WAWANEIKA TROPHY | |
|---|---|
| 1954 | David Moffat |
| 1955 | Nancy McLennan |
| 1956 | Libby Reid |
| 1957 | John Stuart |
| 1958 | Jamee Wadsworth |
| 1959 | Dodie Hodgins, Norm Moffat & Peter Moffat |
| 1960 | Peter Moffat |
| 1961 | John Glendinning |
| 1962 | John Glendinning |
| 1963 | Judy Sissons |
| 1964 | Don Glendinning |
| 1965 | Reid Hudson |
| 1966 | Reid Hudson |
| 1967 | Reid Hudson |
| 1968 | Jim Cruickshank |
| 1969 | David Thompson |
| 1970 | Rob Moffat |
| 1971 | John Eastmure |
| 1972 | John Eastmure |
| 1973 | Ross Hudson |
| 1974 | Ross Hudson, T.L. Moffat & Rick Sieber |
| 1975 | Ross Hudson |
| 1976 | Ross Hudson |
| 1977 | Peter Hughes |
| 1978 | Gordon Moffat |
| 1979 | Eric Lind |
| 1980 | John Moffat |
| 1981 | Scott Fingler |
| 1982 | Graeme Eastmure |
| 1983 | David R. Moffat |
| 1984 | Spencer Todd & Rob Brenciaglia |
| 1985 | Will Holloway |
| 1986 | (name missing) |
| 1987 | Jamie Stuart |
| 1988 | Andrew Moffat |
| 1989 | Andrew Moffat |
| 1990 | Andrew Moffat |
| 1991 | Andrew Moffat |
| 1992 | Andrew Moffat |

## MUSSELMAN TROPHY

An older trophy, this is presented for one of the most popular regatta events, the Ladies' Double Canoe. The Musselman family purchased the Hall cottage in the 1930s and has been on the lake since then. George Musselman served the regatta for a number of years as a starter.

## A.S. PURDY & A.K. PURDY CHALLENGE TROPHY

This trophy was given in memory of Alexander S. Purdy, and his son, Alexander Kirkwood Purdy, who died in 1938. Alexander Kirkwood's name does not appear on the trophy, nor does the word "swimming," for which the trophy is presented.

The earliest plaque on the trophy commemorates the 1940–1941 win by Vesta Rudolph. In those days the swimming race followed a long course — from the Springsyde dock to the present-day Eastmure dock. Vesta Rudolph's win is notable in that she was competing with men. Today this trophy is presented for Men's Swimming.

Judy (Purdy) Maunder, A.S. Purdy's granddaughter, died in 1991. For many years the regatta awards ceremony was held on the lawn of her Springsyde cottage.

## REID SISTERS TROPHY

The Reid sisters are Nancy, Libby, and Cathy, daughters of Eleanor and Buzz Reid, who once owned the C.L. Moffat cottage. The trophy is given for the Girls' Single Canoe.

While the family no longer summers on Penlake, the girls are remembered for their active participation in the regatta. Nancy organized all the events one year, and Cathy's name appears frequently on the Women's Senior Championship trophy.

## RUDOLPH TROPHY

As competition at the annual regatta increased, several trophies, including the Rudolph Trophy, were given specifically to honour female contenders. First presented in 1965, the Rudolph trophy was awarded by Vesta (Rudolph) Edwards for Women's Swimming.

The daughter of Mr. and Mrs. Herbert Rudolph of Springsyde, Vesta often competed in swimming events with men — and won.

## SPURR MEMORIAL TROPHY

Given in 1985 by Dibbie Spurr Appleton in memory of her parents, this trophy is a silver bowl mounted on a wooden base and is the much-sought prize for the Mixed Double Scull. Arthur Clinton "Clint" Spurr, a past president of the association, was an avid golfer who once scored a 29 on the nine-hole Penlake Farms Golf Course. He married Margaret Brown in 1926 in the Brown cottage on Penlake.

## TAYLOR-HUTCHINSON TROPHY

Her own interest in the sport motivated Mary Taylor Hutchinson to give this trophy in 1987 for the Ladies' Double Scull. She honours the memory of her father, a Toronto engineer who in 1919 built the Wee Neuke cottage near Fisher's Point.

## TODD-WADSWORTH TROPHY

The marriage of Thomas Todd and Jamee Wadsworth joined two families with longtime Penlake associations. Tom served for many years as an announcer for portions of the regatta events, and Jamee has been a frequent winner of the Women's Senior Championship. The Todd-Wadsworth Trophy was first presented in 1987 for the Mixed Double Scull, fifteen and under.

*ISA*

# OTHER EVENTS AND TROPHIES

Not all Penlake competitions have taken place at the regatta. Besides the old Penlake Farms Golf Club matches and the weekly sailing races, all of which awarded trophies to winners, there have been many strange and not-so-strange contests: the Toad Race at Springsyde; the Grassy Island Two-ball Mixed Four-some, sponsored by Lamon-McCann; and the Annual Croquet Championship Trophy, presented by David and Margaret Kennard.

Ian and Liz White have held a number of Great White Capers on the Isle Dunelg. The annual Frog Jump event was an integral part of the Caper. Each participant brought his or her best frog. The frogs were placed in a large circle drawn on the ground. The owner of the first frog to cross the line was awarded a floppy stuffed frog onto which his or her name was sewn. The frogs were left on the island.

*Penlake Awards trophy time at the Junior Golf Tournament, circa 1951. Left to right: Ben Spurr, the runner-up, with champion, Bill Charlton.*
– Courtesy the Spurr family

The Worm Crawl race was a similar grand occasion. In the days preceding the event, contestants would search for large, healthy worms to take to the party and enter in the race. The winner's trophy was an attractive stuffed fifteen-inch worm with a female fluttering her eyelashes on one end and a male with collar and tie on the other. Winners' name tags were sewn across the middle section of the worm. Trophies for this event and the Frog Jump were returned by the winners for the next year's competition.

*AMD*

# WORKING

## WORKING ON THE LAKE

*Some work brought no pay:*
*Will Holloway on laundry day.*
– Courtesy Dibbie Spurr Appleton

BACK IN THE DAYS when families spent the entire summer at the lake, kids and dogs and all, jobs were much coveted by teenagers. Jobs meant that they could spend the summer at the cottage and, by virtue of being gainfully employed, remain in the family's good graces. It was especially important to find the right job — one that kept you busy, yielded pocket money (perhaps even a little savings), and left you with enough free time to enjoy being on the lake.

Resorts provided ample summer employment. When they were young Penlakers, Susan Moffat and Nancy MacLennan always competed with local residents for resort jobs. Some teenagers commuted by boat or car. Algonquin Park offered a variety of jobs, from working in a camp to staffing the West Gate, as Nancy Charlton did for several summers.

Sandy McIntosh was employed at a lumber mill not far from the family cottage. During one lunch break, he came upon a bear. Being young and curious, Sandy wondered how fast a bear could run and decided to find out. With a well-aimed toss of a stone, he startled the bear and indeed, it began to run — but Sandy had not anticipated the direction the bear would choose. His curiosity was more than satisfied and his athletic prowess thoroughly tested as he sprinted to safety, barely ahead of his pursuer!

Many teens worked at Portage, including Ian Smart, and Peter and Norm Moffat. Because such young men were often pursued by the young women, the gas pump could be a busy place!

As mentioned earlier, many youngsters earned money by caddying at Penlake Farms Golf Club. Some caddied for their parents, and others had special arrangements with steady customers. David Porter caddied for the Spurrs. Mr. Spurr had a regular 9 a.m. foursome, and frequently returned in the afternoon with Marg Spurr and other family members. To see whether they would be coming on a particular afternoon (few cottagers had phones then), David Porter would run out to the hill on the eighth fairway to check the Spurr boathouse. If a white flag were flying, it meant he could caddy for someone else. Some lads were not much larger than the bags they carried. When golf carts came into fashion, they eased the load, but also lightened the tips. Lugging a heavy bag with a few well-timed moans ensured a much fuller pocket!

Golf-course owners Bill McCready and Emmy (McCready) Sieber frequently hired teens to assist in the office. Jennifer Crabtree worked there for one summer, and Kate (Holloway) Fusco for two. During slow hours, McCready kept them busy removing stubborn weeds from the greens.

A daring young few in need of spending money made occasional late-night forays into the frog pond braving leeches as they retrieved dozens of golf balls mired in the sluggish bottom. The finders would then negotiate a good price for their labours the next day, and the balls would be sold as seconds.

Babysitting has always been an excellent source of spending money. Some teens came to Penlake as nannies while others made themselves available to a number of cottagers.

In addition to caddying and babysitting, I earned money making "cigarettes" which my mother kindly purchased. They were made of pine needles wrapped in one-ply toilet paper. Because no two were the same length, I called them Varieties. I smoked a few myself. You had to be very careful, as they burned so swiftly you could easily burn your lips! I'm sure Mother threw them out, but she bought enough for me to buy a nickel ice-cream cone at Portage. Anna Mirrette Darling says she and Emmy Sieber were in the cigarette trade, too, but using corn silk. "We didn't get paid for ours, though," she adds. "We smoked them all."

Michael Weaber worked at Blackburn's Marina one summer, commuting by boat each day. His father, Dr. William Weaber, often claimed that his son spent more money getting to and from work than he earned all summer! Mollie and Martha Lamon offered a house-maintenance service one summer, as did Kate (Holloway) Fusco and Heather Fraser — though the Holloway-Fraser team may have spent more time sunning on the dock than washing cottage windows!

Whitney Holloway, Nancy Charlton, and Jennifer Garrow served at the ladies' luncheons for many years. Whitney also served at dinner parties. "The pay was okay but I always got a good dinner, too," she remembers. At cocktail parties, young men have worked as dock boys, manoeuvring difficult landings and double-parking boats, as well as assisting women to alight from a moving boat onto a dock with high-heel-sized cracks. Those same young men frequently doubled as bartenders, sometimes mixing a few for themselves in the process.

For a number of years John and Dick Eastmure ran a cottage-maintenance service, which included mowing, staining, painting, repairs, and clearing. Later, Philip and Graeme Eastmure, cousins of the founders, grew into the service and named it Penlake Maintenance. They sent out flyers to people on a select mailing list and were kept busy for several summers. Heather Fraser joined the staff one summer.

Other teens have taught swimming and provided day care. For several years in the 1970s Debbie (Eastmure) Court held a six-week outdoor program on the Isle Dunelg. She and a couple of cohorts also offered crafts, games, picnics, and even an overnight camping experience on Fairy Lake's Lone Tree Island.

In the 1960s the women's committee sponsored a successful Red Cross swim-

*1978 dock repairs*
– Courtesy Anna Mirrette Darling

ming program. Several talented young swimmers, including Mary Rae Cloutier, Linda Mansell, Sherry, and Carol and Judy Sissons, were instructors.

Some teenagers worked at nearby camps enabling them to "get back to the lake" on occasion. Joan (Eastmure) Pratt recalls teaching sailing at Camp Onawa on Lake Vernon. "I'd arrange an overnight sailing trip to Penlake," she remembers. "All the campers stayed at our cottage."

Teens have cut brush, mowed grass, washed dishes, changed diapers, run errands, built docks, and even picked up garbage just to be at the lake. Will Holloway, after being certified for scuba diving, opened Dive and Find, an underwater retrieval service. Colourful posters advertised his skills at a number of lodges. He received calls to recover lost items, mostly jewellery. In addition to a prized Rolex watch, perhaps the most unusual find was a set of false teeth that fell from the wearer's mouth off a government dock. A Huntsville fishing service hired him to retrieve a valuable rod and reel lost over the Portage Rocks. The owner of the *Miss White Pines* tourist boat approached him in a futile attempt to locate a brass propeller, which had gone missing on one of the boat's last runs through Penlake.

Many Penlakers worked on Lang Moffat's farm, which previously belonged to Tom Shaw. Tom Shaw's hired hands often received help from such cottagers as Ian Eastmure, whose family cottage bordered one of the fields where sheep did most of the haying! Joan (Eastmure) Pratt often visited the farm. She reflects: "I remember Bessie [Mrs. Shaw] inviting me in to have lunch with them. Lunch was really dinner on the farm, the main meal of the day. For dessert, she gave us each a big cereal bowl, full of home-tapped maple syrup. I was wondering what it was for when she put out a huge plate of tea biscuits to dip into the syrup!"

Until Shaw sold Wonderview Farm to Moffat, Bill Charlton and Ray Sneyd helped with the haying. So did Ben Spurr and Lang Moffat III. Charlton recalls: "Before they had a baler and modern equipment, haying took most of the summer. It had to be mowed, then turned by hand to dry on both sides. When dry enough, it was loaded loose on a large, flatbed wagon. Once Ray and I were riding on top of a huge load when the tractor rounded the bend at the creek and the load shifted and spilled. We were buried completely in hay until they dug us out. A huge fork-like machine lifted the big loads off the truck and into the barn. They stored the hay loose, not in bales. Heck! When they talk about 'a roll in the hay,' they weren't talking about bales!"

*ISA*

124

***Trail ride at Uncle Lang's***
– Photo by Susan Brenciaglia

# WORKING ON THE FARM

I ADORED POP (my name for Lang Moffat). I don't remember either of my grand-fathers, and because the Moffats treated me like one of the family over the seven summers I worked there in the 1970s, I felt that knowing Pop was as close as I was ever going to come to knowing a grandfather. He had a wry sense of humour and could be gentle and generous. He also could be quick-tempered and irate.

My work involved a lot more than just being "hay crew." Eleven horses — Queenie, Bess, Silver, Stormy, Prince, Duke, Chief, Minnie, Pal, Leo and Christie — all required daily care. I fed and brushed them down, cleaned their hooves, curried them, and mucked out their stalls. That was hard, dirty work. The worst mucking-out job, however, was the sheep barn, a task done every other year. I did it once with Jennifer Garrow, another time with Gord Moffat, and still another time with Nancy Charlton. Over two years the sheep barn, a small, one-storey structure behind the main barn, would build up about a foot of droppings, which had to be shovelled and removed from the premises. The job took a few days but felt like weeks! Sheep are so docile, and so productive!

The first year, I stayed with the Boon family, who lived on the Moffat farm. The Boons helped Pop with the farm all year round.

After summer rides began, I didn't have as much horse care because Pop expected his riders to care for their mounts themselves. Most knew what to do, such as cleaning out the "frog" on a horse's hoof so that nothing was wedged there that could cause lameness or rot. When the rides were over, the horses were wiped down and the tack put away or aired.

The Moffats were very generous, providing daily rides for family and friends, as well as to some local youths. Those rides will long be remembered by those for-tunate enough to have loped through the bush or participated in the Moffats' famous "musical rides" on the great lawn.

Pop kept a few steers, too. After one particularly difficult attempt to round them up at the end of the season, he stabled the steers in the Shaw barn from then on, so that barn, too, had to be mucked out and the animals fed.

Haying season is, by far, the busiest time of summer. Its success depends upon the weather. There must be enough early rain to grow a good crop and there must be warm, sunny days to ripen the hay. The hay must stay dry during haying until it is "back-packed" into the barns. Fermenting hay can result in dangerous spon-taneous combustion.

If it rains after the hay has been cut, it must be turned to dry. If it rains after the hay has been baled, the bales must be stacked — we called it "stooking" — with three bales on end and room for air to circulate. If the bales are too wet, they have to be opened to dry.

Timber wolves waited and watched for small prey while we worked one of the

*The "hay crew" at Wonderview Farm.*
*Left to right: Whitney Holloway,*
*Lang (Pop) Moffat III, Paula Boon,*
*Mark Boon, Will Holloway,*
*Rob Brenciaglia, Tim Moffat,*
*and Scott Musselman.*
– Courtesy Whitney Holloway

"inner" fields toward the trout stream and mountain. As their habitats were destroyed or disturbed, hundreds of field mice scurried about to escape the jaws of the baler. The wolves emerged from the woods to line the perimeter, never straying far from cover. They waited for us to leave, but an occasional flurry in a distant corner was proof that even wolves get impatient.

Bales are loaded onto a wagon by hand. One person on board positions the bales while the crew gathers them and hoists them up. You had to hoist a forty-five to sixty-pound bale six bales up onto the load. The weight depended upon whether it was green or not. After the loss of Pop's old barn to a hay fire, an instrument was used to measure the moisture of the bales. With practice, Pop and his crews knew when the hay was right for storage. By season's end we all sported a good set of "haying muscles."

When rain threatened to spoil a cut field or we found out that help would not be available the next day, we'd all go home for dinner and return to work by the truck headlights.

At the barn, bales were offloaded and ready for back-packing, which is the art of placing the bales in a crisscross stacking pattern, packed tightly, in the loft. At the "new" barn on Highway 60, a conveyor belt helped get the hay into the loft; at the "old" barn, back power did the work. As a good back-packer, I often remained in the top of the barn, where the temperature sometimes reached a hundred degrees Fahrenheit.

Haying was hot, heavy, back-breaking work. You got hay in your eyes, your nose, your mouth, even in your ears. Over the years some of the people who ate hay right along with me were, in addition to Moffat grandsons Ross, T.L. and Gord, all the Boon kids — Mark, Paula, and Heather — and their dad, Glen Boon. When Glen worked, he was in charge, even in the summers when Pop called me the foreman. Others were John and Jennifer Garrow, Rob and Chrissy Brenciaglia, Will Holloway, Mike Sneyd, Curt and Scott Musselman, Tim Moffat, and all the Charltons — Nancy, Greg, Ted, and Howard. Phil and Graeme Eastmure helped out. Helpers in other years included Alan Kennard, Rupert Ambler, Rick Walker, Ross Hudson, Stuart Lamon, Norm Moffat, and Peter Moffat. There were probably twice that number in total. Haying was a big summertime job at the lake.

We laughed, joked, and urged each other on. There was always music, and we'd sing, talk in funny voices, and tell jokes, many of them unprintable. We'd talk about what we were going to be when we grew up. It was very satisfying work, and in fact, many of us did grow up right there on Pop's farm.

Gord Moffat recalls, "In a summer, the hay crew took about 2,000 to 3,000 bales off the fields to the barns; another 2,000 or more got sold right off the field."

It was a wonderful experience for me. I can still smell the hay, the sweet grass, newly mowed. Memories of those days are precious.

*Whitney Holloway*

*Disabled children often came to ride at Wonderview Farm, circa 1986.*
– Courtesy Whitney Holloway

127

# DEERHURST IN THE EARLY 1960s

IN its organization and ambience Deerhurst Inn of three decades ago resembled the 1890s more than the 1990s! Maurice and Jean Waterhouse operated the inn from May 24th until Labour Day. A marvellous landscape painter, Mr. Waterhouse invited fellow artists to the Inn for a week at the end of September to capture the incredible fall colours.

The staff consisted of a cook and her assistant, a pastry cook, two salad girls/dishwashers, seven waitresses, two office workers, and a maintenance man and his assistant. The waitresses served three meals a day, six days a week, catering to the

*Aerial photo of Deerhurst with the Wadsworth cottages at the lakeside.*
– Courtesy the Spurr family

same families throughout their holidays. Besides setting tables, they did chambermaid duties between breakfast and lunch. However, they joined everyone at the dock in the afternoon. In addition to a weekly salary, the waitresses were tipped generously by the families they had served.

Job interviews were very difficult! In 1960, attired in a wet bathing suit, I walked up to the front desk and asked Mr. Waterhouse for a job the next year. We agreed that I would start work on the May holiday weekend. I rejoined my friends to ski back to Springsyde.

As part of the office staff, I looked after the front desk in the morning and evening one day, and the afternoon the next, seven days a week. Everyday duties included maintaining guests' accounts, sorting the mail, typing the daily menus, ordering and receiving supplies, and acting as dining-room hostess when guests arrived for meals. Since the office had the only phone on the property, I received all calls, delivered messages, and placed long-distance calls, the most memorable being a call to Mr. Robert MacNamara, the president of the World Bank. One perk enjoyed by the office staff was an occasional invitation to a cocktail party at a cottage.

In addition to single rooms in the inn, the one- to five-bedroom cottages nestled in the trees accommodated about ninety people. Wonderful home-style meals were served at precise hours: breakfast from eight to nine, lunch twelve-thirty to one, and dinner six-thirty to seven. Dresses and jackets with ties were *de rigueur* at dinnertime. During my years at Deerhurst, the only person to break the code was actor Bruno Gerussi, who was at the time a star of the Stratford Festival. With family in tow, he ate in a sport shirt and sandals.

Families who stayed for a month or more often had boats, which were stored at Blackburn's in winter. Teenagers became part of the lake gang. Golfers honed their skills for small wagers on the side lawn putting green. Regulars played highly competitive billiard games nightly on the old English billiard table. Organized inn activities were minimal: an evening beach barbecue, a picnic at Flat Rock, and the annual two-ball foursome golf tournament at the Penlake Farms Golf Club.

I spent four wonderful summers at Deerhurst Inn, commuting from my family's cottage by boat or car. Driving presented a unique challenge. If I didn't get through Farnsworth's farm by 7:50 a.m., I had to wait while the herd of cows ambled across the road and into the barn, and I would be late for breakfast.

The Deerhurst of today is a wondrous and exciting place. But I still fondly remember the relaxed camaraderie of owners, staff, and guests at the Deerhurst of the 1960s.

*Nancy MacLennan Rogers*

# POTPOURRI

## PENINSULA LAKE ASSOCIATION

*The Penlake Association letterhead*

Cottagers' associations have existed on Peninsula Lake since the turn of the century. The first, the Springsyde Cottagers' Association, was organized in 1905 and still exists. There was a Hillside Association in the 1940s, which served the interests of small groups of cottagers, and as such worked very well.

In the early 1930s, however, the growing summer population required a more representative group.

The North Muskoka Lakes Association (NMLA) was formed in 1935 to represent cottagers on the four Huntsville lakes: Vernon, Mary, Fairy, and Peninsula. The members of the executive were drawn from each lake. The association met regularly until 1942, then didn't meet again until the end of the war.

In 1948 it was decided that each lake was to form its own branch with its own constitution and bank account to exercise better financial control over its obligations to the parent body. At the time, Peninsula Lake was providing seventy-five per cent of the fees to the NMLA.

And so the North Muskoka Lakes Association, Peninsula Lake branch, was formed, drafting its own constitution along the lines of the NMLA and agreeing to assist it financially. This arrangement gave the branch associations better control of local affairs.

The NMLA was gradually phased out in later years. In 1979 the Peninsula Lake Association was fortunate to have a very enthusiastic ladies' committee, which took over the social membership at the Penlake Farms Golf Club and organized numerous events.

In 1953 the association took responsibility for the annual Penlake regatta. The regatta, the premier summer event, is a major financial undertaking.

The association has been involved in many lake issues, including the perennial problem of water levels. If water levels are too low, people cannot use their boathouses; if they are too high, docks and shore structures are severely damaged. In the 1940s Bracebridge Hydro was often accused of drawing down our lakes to provide Bracebridge with cheap power rather than purchasing it from Ontario Hydro. Poor controls in years of unusually great spring runoff have also been a problem, about which the association executive has had frequent meetings with various government departments. Although the present system of controlling lake levels is not infallible, improvements have been made.

The unsafe operation of powerboats has been a recurring problem. The 1945 annual meeting debated the need for courtesy by the operators of large boats to smaller crafts and canoes, particularly in the canal. In recent years, the association has attempted to control fast, noisy racing boats, which have become something of a menace.

The purity of lake water has always been a concern. In 1939 the sanitary committee of the association arranged with the engineering branch of the provincial Department of Health to do a house-to-house inspection on the four lakes to test the water, and examine sanitary conveniences and garbage-disposal practices. A similar inspection was carried out recently on Peninsula Lake. A number of cottages were required to update antiquated septic systems.

The association closely monitored the expansion of the large resorts in the west end of the lake during the 1970s and 1980s. Until the resorts were hooked up to the Huntsville sewage system, sewage lagoons sometimes overflowed into the lake. At one point treated effluent was actually discharged by a pipe into the lake bottom at Deerhurst Bay.

In 1970 the boundaries for the proposed District of Muskoka municipality were being determined. The Town of Huntsville proposed that the whole of Peninsula Lake be included within its boundaries; as recipient of development taxes, it would encourage the updating and enlarging of resorts. But the association was negotiating with the minister of the Ontario Department of Municipal Affairs to have Peninsula Lake included within the boundaries of the Township of Lake of Bays. A compromise was finally reached. The larger eastern portion of the lake was included within the Lake of Bays; the smaller western portion was allocated to the Town of Huntsville.

In 1973 a new bridge over the canal was proposed. The association executive negotiated with the Ministry of Transport to ensure that the bridge was tall enough for Albacore sailboats to be towed through the canal for weekly races in Mary and Fairy lakes. It took until 1991 to build this structure!

The Peninsula Lake Association has served the interests of its members well. It is indebted to past and present executive members for helping to make Penlake such a pleasant alternative to the busy, noisy cities where most of us live.

*Russell Eastmure*

# LADIES' COMMITTEE

In 1929 THE PENLAKE FARMS GOLF CLUB sold social memberships for its inaugural season for five dollars apiece. Social members could use the clubhouse and attend entertainments, including buffet suppers, corn roasts, and luncheons. A Monte Carlo Night featured exotic dancing by a young cottager; some members were scandalized!

The weekly ladies' bridge party was the most popular and longest-lasting event. Members took turns providing sandwiches and little cakes and performed the chore of tea hostess, which entailed pouring tea from a stylish urn. They also paid a weekly fee for purchasing prizes, playing cards, tallies, teaspoons, bridge tables, and bridge chairs. This self-sufficient group had its own bank account in Huntsville until 1980. After the incorporation of the Peninsula Lake Association, the social group became the Peninsula Lake Association Ladies' Committee.

In 1958 several parents requested a Red Cross program to teach swimming and water safety to the children, to occupy their time meaningfully, and to give them the achievement awards that many of their peers won at camp. The North Muskoka Lakes Association, Penlake Branch, inaugurated a swimming program under the auspices of the Ladies' Committee.

For several years there were two programs — one for July and one for August. Enrolment varied between twenty-five and fifty children a season, and approximately eighty per cent passed their final Red Cross examination. Several qualified young people were instructors and assistants at the Purdys' beach on Springsyde. The committee greatly appreciated the co-operation and patience of the Purdy family.

As many participants became graduates and fewer children were spending entire summers at the family cottages, the demand for instruction decreased. Qualified instructors were harder to find for the time frame and limited remuneration. The course was terminated in 1972.

The Ladies' Committee also launched other social activities. Buffet suppers were revived each July, attracting up to two hundred people. As many as five turkeys were cooked at various households. Volunteers provided all the vegetables, salads, and desserts. The Hillside Ladies' Auxiliary, including such familiar names as Tapley, Thompson, McQuirter, Higgins, Hill, and Cotterchio, helped serve the dinner and cleaned up afterward.

The corn roast was reinstated and held beside the old number-one fairway of the golf club. Committee volunteers convened the event. George McQuirter cooked the corn in a large, black, maple-syrup kettle over an open fire; he was assisted by Sam Wright, who was also in charge of docking boats. Non-members of the association had to pay: seventy-five cents for adults, twenty-five cents for children. An ever-popular baseball game pitted the men against the "young fellows."

Children's games were organized. After the roast families enjoyed a singsong and square dancing to the calls of Ross Ennest in the pavilion.

Children loved the annual masquerade party, which kept families scurrying around for novel costumes.

A junior committee bolstered teenage participation in Penlake events as an alternative to travelling late at night to Huntsville by car or boat and the dangers inherent therein. The teenagers assisted at the regatta, arranged dance parties at the pavilion (George Musselman provided the music on his PA system), and shucked corn for the corn roast.

In 1960 the ladies' bridge group merged with the program committee. Approximately thirty members and their guests enjoyed potluck luncheons in July and August. Since then, the women's annual meeting has been held at the August luncheon. After 1966 the Tuesday bridge teas at the clubhouse were discontinued. Potluck luncheons carried on until fire destroyed the clubhouse in 1972. Since then members have graciously offered their cottages.

Latterly, the ladies' committee has been providing coffee and doughnuts before the annual meeting of the Peninsula Lake Association. At times attendance at these meetings has been more than a hundred.

*AMD*

# MUSICAL TALENTS

Penlake has had its share of musical talent. Fred Sylvester, whose cottage was near Pow Wow Point, was the registrar of the Royal Conservatory of Music for many years and the conductor of the Mendelssohn Choir from 1957 to 1960. His wife, Eve, taught the Orff method of music to schoolchildren.

Frequently they had as their house guest Lois Marshall, one of Canada's most outstanding artists. Her talent, which allowed her a successful international career as a recitalist and a concert and opera soloist, made for many an exciting musical evening at the Sylvester cottage. Their guests included Jack Hodgins, the choirmaster of Grace Church-on-the-Hill and the Bishop Strachan School Choir. At one time, composer Geoffrey Ridout owned the cottage next door.

There have been many musically talented cottagers on Penlake, including concert soloist Ida McLean Dilworth, soloist Si Hodgins (a wonderfully enthusiastic song leader at social gatherings!), chorister Bea Joy Charlton McBrien, and pianist May Henderson Ruckert. Both the Bullen daughters, Billie Potter and Bea Gordon, are gifted musicians. Bea plays the organ for the Pioneer Memorial Church at Hillside. We've also enjoyed Jean Rogers on the accordion, Russ Smart on the ukulele, Ian and Don Eastmure on the bagpipes, among others.

*AMD*

*Ladies' luncheon at Janet Irwin's.*
*Left to right: Janet Irwin, Pat Lamon,*
*Joan Sissons-Beatty, and*
*Margaret Moffat (Mrs. Norman).*
– Courtesy Margaret (Mrs. Robert) Moffat

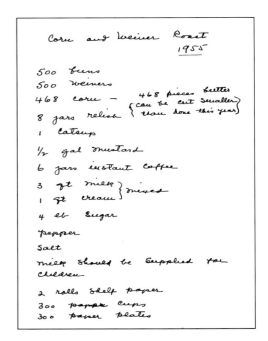

*A corn roast shopping list*
– Courtesy Mary Weaber

133

## THE VICTROLA

*"Mommy, what's a Victrola?"*

Mommy's eyes took on a faraway look and her face softened, as old memories flooded back. Finally she answered, "A Victrola is a phonograph machine. Your mommy had a portable one at the cottage as a little girl. Sometimes she would put the Victrola in her canoe with her favourite records and paddle out into the lake to soak up the sun and listen to her special songs. The only problem was that she had to keep winding the spring on the turntable with a little crank to keep it turning.

"When your mommy was a little older, she would sometimes go out in the canoe at night with one of her many boyfriends. The boy would paddle the canoe, and Mommy would sit in the bottom, leaning against a back rest, and put their favourite records on the Victrola, all the while cranking up the spring.

"When your daddy asked your mommy to marry him, they were paddling home from the regatta dance. The night was warm and quiet, there was a full moon reflecting across the water, and we had just finished playing our favourite song on the Victrola when he popped the question. Ah yes, the Victrola..."

*RDM*

## SQUARE DANCING

At one time square dancing was an important weekly social event for the locals. The little community halls bounced to the music and the stomping of feet. The spirit was often assisted with some good homemade dandelion wine. Dancing stopped at midnight when the women brought out sandwiches, cake, and coffee. After the food was devoured, everyone joined in song. The evening was capped off with one last square.

Bob Wright sometimes held hoedowns in his living room, and Joe Bullen in his boathouse.

As the years went on, more and more cottagers joined in, and became as proficient as the local people. With improved transportation, you could go to a different dance every night of the week. Even the Peninsula Lake Association got caught up in the swing and sponsored a square dance every Saturday night at the golf club pavilion.

The many callers all developed their individual styles. One caller would mouth the sound of steel brushes on the drums while another might see if he could catch the dancers napping by mixing up the calls. How often did we hear, "Allemande ...allemande...allemande RIGHT with your opposite across the floor!" And the shouts and hurrahs when the caller said, "Ladies cross their lily-white hands, gents their black-and-tan..."? This dance originally had the ladies linking hands over the necks of the gents, and the gents linking theirs around the waists of the ladies,

*Square dance at the pavilion, Whitney Holloway and Ross Moffat in the foreground.*
– Courtesy Whitney Holloway

*"Lily-white-hands," Penlake-style.*
*Jennifer Garrow on the left and*
*Mollie Lamon on the right.*
– Courtesy Whitney Holloway

while they pivoted gently to the music. Occasionally the beat, and therefore the pivoting, would speed up, and unless the ladies were leaning well back, their feet might begin to slip from the centre. If the swing continued to speed up, the feet, legs, and bodies of the ladies might fly out parallel to the floor.

One night, at one of the golf club dances, one woman did become airborne. She lost her grip on her neighbour's hand and went flying out through the screened window of the pavilion to land unceremoniously amongst the trees. After that, gallant young gentlemen decided to link their arms to cradle all the ladies and swing them together. This is a practice quite unique to Penlake, we believe.

There's not a lot of square dancing going on around the lake these days, but the best one in recent years — early 1970s, I believe — was the lively square dance at Judy Sisson's wedding reception — so lively, in fact, we feared the cottage might bounce off its foundation!

*RDM*

# LOVE

**Love and kisses**
– Courtesy Mom

OLD CARS WITH THEIR RUMBLE SEATS and the newer flashy convertibles cruising the streets were usually good bait for a young woman looking for romance. However, nothing could equal the sight of a sleek craft under full sail gliding swiftly up to a crowded resort dock where it would be brought into the wind at the last possible moment to rest quietly alongside.

"Anyone for a sail?" the young yachtsman would call.

Fortunate indeed were those teenagers lucky enough to have access to a sailboat. For what better way to spend a beautiful summer day than sailing into Fairy Lake, maybe even into Huntsville, with newfound friends? Who could possibly be faulted if on the way home the wind died with the setting sun? With the cool offshore breezes coming down from the hills, how could one possibly keep warm, except by huddling closely together and sharing body heat?

I'm sure many have experienced similar innocent adventures. It is the memories of the crazy things one does as a teenager that help make Penlake the very special place it is in the hearts of all of us.

*RDM*

## SOUNDS OF PENLAKE

*A loon*

REMEMBER THE TOOT OF THE LITTLE TRAIN and the dramatic squeak of the wheels as it rounded Osborne Lake? Remember the awesome sound of the deep, reverberating whistle of the *Algonquin* warning smaller crafts of her presence in the canal? (If you were in a boat, it was wise to head for the nearest exit.) And who can ever forget the Tally Ho bugle announcing breakfast, lunch, and dinner at the hotel? Or the rumble of the miniature cannon Mr. Dilworth fired at sunset from the end of his dock. And on still mornings, the clinking of cowbells from the distant hills.

Those of us on shores buffeted by the prevailing west winds know well the crash of waves on the rocks, the rattle of the dock rings, and the banging of the boats against the dock as they rise and fall in a storm. The wind rustles in the trees. The songs of birds surround us. The loon calls hauntingly to its mate on a still night.

And the peaceful silence of Penlake...

*AMD*

# MEMORIALS

Over the years several Penlakers have been honoured with unobtrusive memorials.

A spring on the edge of what was the second fairway of the Penlake Farms Golf Club yields delicious cool water. It was a favourite of many golfers, who often left their bags and carts unattended while they lingered at the spring for a refreshing drink. When Gene Henderson, an avid golfer, died, his wife, May, had the structure around the spring repaired and improved in his memory.

Friends of Frank Hubble along the Tally Ho shore requested that a highway sign be placed in his memory on the road to his cottage. It reads, "Hubble's Lane."

Agnes Moffat McGee placed a plaque on her cottage at Springsyde in memory of her husband, Dr. Rusty McGee.

Margaret Moffat dedicated a window in the historic little Stewart Memorial United Church at Dwight: "In Loving Memory of Norman Douglas Moffat." The church is located a mile from Shadow Rock Farm and the cottage he loved.

Bryce Moffat raised daylilies and even cultivated his own variety called Springsyde, which is a beautiful, yellow early-blooming plant. After his death, his widow, Peg, offered daylilies to cottagers around the lake. We all refer to them as Bryce's lilies.

Eve Silvester loved flowers, but her cottage was in a shady spot on the Pow Wow shore. Nevertheless, she was able to grow beautiful Shasta daisies. She gave me a clump, which took hold and spread at my place. I have given many roots to Penlakers, and the daisies have travelled around the lake in her memory.

*AMD*

*Flowers, a living memorial*
– Courtesy Anna Mirrette Darling

# NATURE AND THE COTTAGER

The forces of nature certainly play a greater role at the cottage than they do in the city. Most Torontonians, for instance, are not bothered by submerged rocks, high water, and destructive waves.

Yet cottages are often less well constructed than city dwellings. Many Penlake cottages were built almost a century ago. The original builders never intended them to last forever, nor could they have envisioned their descendants adding onto, shoring up, and forever maintaining their age-old places in an annual ritual. "Grandmother would have wanted it this way!" we protest. But Grandmother would have been stunned to know that the taxes on the land on which she built are greater today than her original purchase price!

Unfortunately, though, the older a cottage gets, the more susceptible it is to the whims of nature. Consider clay. While not an *act* of nature, clay is certainly a *fact* of nature. The land on which many Penlake cottages are built is composed largely of clay. Each year the ever-wary cottager, returning for a summer's sojourn,

*A boat surrounded in smoke haze caused by the forest fires in 1913.*
– Courtesy T.L. Moffat

*Winoka Shore - casualty*
*of the prevailing wind.*
– Courtesy Anna Mirrette Darling

may be greeted by unwelcome surprises. If built on clay, an unwinterized cottage that shifts with the heaving frost may not return to its original position. An annual levelling is required. Owners of such cottages become used to cockeyed doors and gently rolling floors, and experience difficulty walking normally in a level cottage.

Tent caterpillars have wreaked havoc in the woods around Muskoka's cottages. Cottagers themselves have endured invasions of bats, bees, carpenter ants, mice, birds (in chimneys), sheep, and other uninvited visitors. They've exterminated, sprayed, set traps, and shored up. In the end, they simply shrug and say, "That's cottage life!"

Like all the Muskoka lakes, Penlake has had its share of violent weather. In the 1950s a freak windstorm, officially labelled a cyclone, tore through the area, uprooting beautiful, century-old trees — such as the lone pine for which Thomas Lang Moffat named the rocky point near his cottage. Heavy rains have submerged docks and water pumps. On the east shore, high water causes Frenchman's Creek to flood the farm road.

A lack of rain is equally alarming, especially in the 1990s, with our understanding of global warming and the "greenhouse effect." Cottagers understand how precious our water supply is and how we must conserve it.

The lake level affects not only boating, but the domestic water supply, as most

*High water at the Springsyde dock*
– Courtesy Dorothy Mansell Eastmure

cottages are plumbed by lake intakes. The water level certainly affects ecology, from plant growth to fish-hatching to the activity of micro-organisms at the lake bottom. But rain, or the lack thereof, is only partially responsible for the level of Penlake.

Locks on the water system also control the lake level; some years, they have determined the prevailing conditions. During one particularly hot summer in the 1950s the locks were opened to permit more water to reach the lower lakes, robbing Peter to pay Paul. On Penlake, many cottagers found their big wooden boats sitting on dry land in the boathouse while boaters on Lake Muskoka enjoyed a higher lake level. Slips were dredged to get the boats out of the boathouse into deeper water, or the boats were hoisted on pulleys and lake access given up. In those days, boats were not only recreational vehicles, but the primary mode of transport from one place to another, as many cottages did not yet have road access.

Not all the natural phenomena on Penlake are as clearly visible as low water or wind-toppled trees. The lake harbours formidable rock hazards. While there are some that can be seen easily, such as the Portage rocks and the grassy islands at the entrance to Hill's Bay, others can not be seen at all. At the entrance to Wolf Bay are a number of shoals, and the formation known as "twin rocks" on the east shore — off what used to be called Brown's Point — has been particularly harsh on boats; these two enormous boulders, submerged about a foot below the surface, are scarred by the passing of unwary craft. Buoys mark the rocks, but strong winds from the west and big waves make it difficult to see the buoys!

Most native Penlakers know where the rocks are, but when they marry an outsider, that person is sure to be the recipient of repeated lectures, mostly from in-laws, about the dangers of Penlake's rocks. This ritual follows a courtship, often well past the honeymoon, until at long last begrudging permission to use the family boat is granted. In some instances the permission never comes.

The concern for submerged hazards led one small group of spouses to form a select club. The "I Don't Know Where the Damn Rocks Are" Club was founded by Gordon Pratt and Buzzy Lind. Both married longtime Penlakers, Joan Eastmure and Patsy Hardie respectively.

Howdy Marshall, married to Penny Spurr, was also a member. Another was Arthur Scully, who married Eleanor "Gishy" Foster and was steadfastly denied permission to skipper Dr. Foster's boat for several years, despite the fact that he served on the aircraft carrier USS *Lake Champlain.* Only one female member, Emily Jarrett, who married Charles "Indy" Jarrett, was inducted into the club.

A heavy fog over water can be devastating to a boater. The fog of late summer comes on with surprising speed, completely disorienting a boater. Ralph Dilworth and his wife, Edith, set forth for home one evening after a game of bridge. "No problem," Ralph assured his hosts. "I have a compass on board and I know the lake like the back of my hand." Two hours later they were back, soaking and shaken, their boat half-sunk on the rocks.

Oh yes, the compass had worked. The boat's direction had been correct. But in the dense fog Ralph did not know just how far across the lake he had progressed. Thinking he had passed between the big island and the golf peninsula, he veered right toward his part of the lake. In fact, the boat had not fully crossed the eastern portion of the lake. He turned the boat straight into Hill's Bay, ramming one of the grassy islands at the entrance to the bay. They were rescued by the Kennards.

Heavy snow is another problem to the cottager. In the spring, when the cottage lies buried beneath a thick white blanket, a sudden warming accompanied by a rainfall can collapse a cottage roof. City dwellers shovel their driveway; cottagers shovel their roofs!

Without a doubt, the greatest fear of nature held by cottagers is of ice. The question "Has the ice gone out yet?" is often the first thing one cottager will ask another when communications are restored after the winter's lull. For those with docks and boathouses, especially ones that face the prevailing winds, the threat of ice damage is a grave concern. Repairs are always costly.

In 1980, however, it didn't matter what shore of Penlake one lived on. With the lack of usual quantities of snow in Muskoka that year, the ground frost was quite severe and thus the spring runoff was abundant. The ground could not absorb the spring rain. The Big East flooded, and everywhere, water was high. Lake

*The power of nature - 1940.*
– Photo by Frank Winterbottom,
courtesy I.S. Appleton

ice was, therefore, borne higher than usual and hit — when it hit — above the strong, rock-filled cribs, high on unprotected boathouse walls.

Damage on Penlake included not just the east shore, where prevailing winds often bring spring ice damage, but all four exposures. Docks large and small were heavily damaged or destroyed. Conservative estimates in the paper calculated half a million dollars in damage on Penlake alone.

Ice makes one truly aware of the power of nature. No bulldozer could have moved my grandmother's dock onto dry land had we so ordered it. But there it sat, fifteen feet up on the shore, trees shoved over!

One spring I came up just as the ice was going out. On the Winoka shore, also an eastern exposure, some of the splintered remains of the sturdy, Petersen-built, two-slip boathouse belonging to Dr. John and Trudy (Spurr) Hay were hanging in trees twenty feet inland! Farther down the shore, the cheerful red roof of the large Foster boathouse lay flat at the water level, silent testimony to the destructive force of wind-driven ice.

The end of our dock had broken off and ridden the ice into the boathouse, acting like a battering ram. It took out the supporting central column and came to rest sideways inside the boathouse with our boats on top!

142

At 6 a.m. our boathouse was still standing, and the boats were still inside. By 10:30 a.m., thanks to Colin Winterbottom of South Portage, Paul Robinson, and Alex Cousintine, the boats were out. The four of us, though I was a very small part of the operation, worked very carefully — like working with nitroglycerine — to ease the boats from the groaning structure.

We'd hoped that strong cables and a winch would save the boathouse. When I took a picture from the third green at the golf course, it was still standing. Colin called me at home in Pittsburgh that night to say that the boathouse had collapsed with an explosive roar around three that afternoon — fifteen minutes after I left the golf course to go home.

Large double structures, like the Foster, Hay, Spurr, and Brown boathouses, were levelled and wrecked as if in the path of a tornado. Even the McEwen boathouse on Wolf Island, sheltered from the flow of ice and protected from winds, was damaged in the ice of 1980. The Dr. Howard Charlton boathouse, built in 1931 in a quiet cove on Hill's Bay, went out with dozens of other sturdy structures, and Don McIntosh, who'd had a new dock built the previous fall, never even got to see it!

A few cottagers in recent years have tried to combat the ice by installing bubblers to keep the water open around the docks. While the principle is a good one, the device is of little use if the winds blow ice across the open water and into your dock. One area resident reports having seen a boathouse on his lake that was virtually destroyed by the action of a bubbler. The open water inside the boathouse created so much moisture in the closed structure that all the walls were blackened by mildew and rot!

Ice and bubblers pose yet another problem, not just to the cottagers, but to freewheeling snowmobilers who race with careless abandon across (not always) frozen lakes. Each year the newspapers carry accounts of accidents where a snowmobile and its rider have gone down on a lake.

A Penlake cottager warned in the spring of 1992 that snowmobiles and bubblers don't mix. While checking the cottage for ice damage, Drew Hudson was relieved to see a certain amount of open water around his boathouse. Several days later, however, with the return of freezing temperatures, the open water was glazed over. What alarmed Hudson was the sight of snowmobile tracks on both sides of the open area!

Some daring snowmobilers are known to leap these open spaces — it's called puddle-hopping. Under proper conditions, with a diver at the ready, this activity can be relatively safe. But on a quiet lake just awakening from winter, puddle-hopping is literally skating on thin ice.

One of the greatest joys of being at the cottage is the feeling of communing with nature. While certainly no longer a wilderness, the lake nevertheless attracts all kinds of wildlife, from the occasional moose to a herd of whitetail deer to the raccoons, which still fare well with leftovers. Several loon families patrol the shores while great blue heron fish from their lofty, long-legged perch. Signs that beaver are alive and well abound, and the lake is a birder's paradise. Countless wildlife — from minks, muskrats, and porcupines, to chipmunks, black bears, and timber wolves — coexist in harmony on the shores of Penlake. Nature is in her glory.

Two faces of nature, each awesome. One gives us the privilege and joy of seeing wildlife on our shores, experiencing a sense of the pioneer spirit and how it must have been before human "progress." The other, over which we have no control — ice, wind, rain, rocks, sun, the earth itself — keeps us on our toes, ever mindful that while it may be cottage country, it's God's country first!

*ISA*

*Seagull at Brown's Point in 1915.*
*Wolf Island is in the background.*
– Courtesy the Spurr family